Christmas
with
Mary Cook

Favourite Stories and Recipes

www.creativebound.com

Published by Creative Bound Inc.
Box 424, Carp, ON
Canada K0A 1L0
(613) 831-3641   info@creativebound.com

ISBN 0-921165-88-9
Printed and bound in Canada

© Mary Cook
© 1997, 1998, 2002, 2006 Creative Bound Inc.

Book design by Wendelina O'Keefe
Cover photo © PhotoDisc

Library and Archives Canada Cataloguing in Publication Data

Cook, Mary
    Christmas with Mary Cook : favourite stories and recipes

ISBN 0-921165-88-9

    1. Christmas stories, Canadian (English).
2. Christmas cookery. I. Title.

PS8555.O566C57 1997   C813'.54   C97-901054-3
PR9199.3.C6397C57 1997

Time to Celebrate!

Since this book was first published almost ten years ago, so much has changed, and yet in many respects, so much has stayed the same. *Christmas with Mary Cook* has gone through several reprints, and along the way has become a Canadian bestseller. It would seem to me, although the world itself has gone through many revisions since that first printing, what has remained constant is the continuing search for the simple joys of life. And so, once again, this very simple book of recipes and stories is reaching out to connect its readers with the joys of another era.

However, since the initial release of *Christmas with Mary Cook*, many changes have taken place in my life, and the lives of those people who fill its pages. My beloved sister Audrey has passed away, and yet her legacy lives on. She will always remain a vital part of my storytelling, and I think she would be happy to know that even though she is no longer here to reminisce with me, I will continue to weave her into my narrations.

My impish cousin Ronny lost his long battle with diabetes, and yet his name alone can bring a smile to the faces of those who loved him, and I will continue to intertwine his antics into my telling of those happy days when life was full of adventure and warmth. His young brother Terry will very likely grow in importance in my stories, and will no doubt fill any void in the stories left by Ronny's passing.

Much has changed in my own life. I now have five grandchildren who live in constant dread that Grammy will somehow weave them into her storytelling, bringing them a notoriety they don't want! Our son Richard continues to live in Indonesia, but comes home often enough that we can keep those cherished family traditions alive that we all cherish. When he does come back to Canada, I bring out all his favourite dishes, most of which can be found in this book, and which are foreign to the land in which he lives.

When this book was first published, our daughter Mary Jane's son was only seven. Now, he is in university. It is heartwarming to me, a traditionalist, that our daughter has kept alive many of the family customs she grew up with. Holidays are still a time for family gatherings, complete with suitable decorations, many of which have been in our family for decades.

Our youngest daughter Melinda is a school teacher, and it is a joy to me that she has continued to adhere to the same work ethics she was taught, and which I was taught before her.

My soulmate Wally, who stood behind me while bringing this, and my other books, to fruition, continues to inspire, support and encourage me in all I do. Even though he has been retired for more than ten years, Wally stands behind my decision, to continue writing my stories as long as I can put two words, coherently, one after the other, and my readers continue to enjoy what I write.

The electronic method I must use today is very different from what I used to put together my very first book more than thirty years ago. The method has changed, but my reason for writing has stayed the same. I think, perhaps, I write as much for myself, as I do for those who enjoy what I create.

And so, yes indeed, things have changed, much in the name of progress. But I feel that I have changed very little. I still cherish my family and friends. My very survival depends on having them beside me in all I do. I still live with a deep faith that gives me strength every day. I still enjoy the simple pleasures that come my way. What more can I ask for?

Merry Christmas!

Contents

Traditions

As a traditionalist who misses so very much the Christmas atmosphere of so many years ago, I can't help but reflect on the holiday season of the 1930s and compare it with the holidays we experience now. When I talk about those lost traditions and what they mean to me, I sometimes find I am searching for a gossamer dream, one that is barely remembered but still there—real, yet elusive. And I wonder if what I am really searching for is the contentment that came from an era when there was no struggle for happiness; it was just there. When it didn't really matter that there wasn't enough money to buy new Christmas decorations, and you made do with last year's coloured paper-chains. When gifts exchanged might be nothing more than one of your own cherished possessions lovingly given up as your way of saying, "I care enough to give to you what is precious to me."

And when I think of a New Year's Eve of another time, I remember how it wasn't important that you weren't included in the community's most prestigious party. You preferred to stay home with your own family, drinking homemade eggnog and singing songs around the old pipe organ. That was where you wanted to be, with the people who were most important to you and with whom you had laughed and cried through another year, and anticipated the months ahead.

As I try to justify the artificial tree that has replaced the spruce hauled from our own bush, I miss the smell of the boughs, and yes, I even miss the job which always fell to me to daily take the broom and dustpan and sweep up the needles that continually fell to the pine floor from the branches that dried out quickly because of the blinding heat of the Findlay Oval and the dryness of the log house made airtight against the winter. Messy and almost bald when we discarded it on New Year's Day, the spruce tree, too, has gone, replaced by one that is fireproof and cleaner and symmetrically perfect and safe, to be packed away in a cardboard box and brought out year after year.

And even though I try, I can never really duplicate my mother's tourtières which we had on Christmas Eve or on New Year's Day for dinner. I use exactly the same ingredients, and I think the proportions are reasonably accurate, but there is always something missing. Perhaps it is that all our hands had a part in the making of those pies in the 1930s. Audrey would roll the crust and Emerson would hold the grinder tight to the table while I fed in the pork. Everett would stoke the stove to make sure the oven was hot. Earl would mix the seasonings with the meat. Even Father would flute the edge of the crusts.

Today I make my pork pies when the house is quiet and the hands on the kitchen clock tell me I should have been in bed long ago if I had any hope of accomplishing what is on my list for tomorrow.

I guess what I miss more than anything are the smells of those holidays of that era. Wet socks and gum rubbers drying out behind the stove at the Christmas concert of the Northcote School; the real tree, of course; choke-cherry jam mixed with horse-radish simmering on the back of the stove for the turkey; mother's special homemade dressing with real summer savoury and raisins; cinnamon cookies in honey pails in the roll-top cupboard; the smell of homemade soap in our hair as it was washed and tied up in rags to be corkscrew-perfect for the holidays.

And yet, even though I become nostalgic when my mind passes over that sweep of memories of those years past, I realize that every day, we as families are building new traditions—traditions and memories that will probably stand the test of time just as those of the Depression years, because who's to say the memories of another time are any more cherished than those that have just been built. The important thing is that we can sort through both the old and the new and keep what is precious, while discarding those that fail to lighten our hearts and cheer our minds.

Mary Cook.

☙ Pork Tourtières ❧

It just wasn't Christmas without tourtières when I was growing up on the farm. They were a special holiday fare which my mother made as part of her French heritage. She used to make the tourtières a week or more before Christmas, wrap them very tightly and store them out in the summer kitchen where they froze solid. They kept very well until needed. Sometimes we served the tourtières on Christmas Eve. Other times we saved them until New Year's Day. This was my mother's favourite recipe.

1 lb.	lean, ground pork	450 g
1 tsp.	salt	5 mL
1/8 tsp.	pepper	.5 mL
1/2 tsp.	celery salt	2 mL
1 large	clove of garlic	1 large
1/4 tsp.	ground cloves	1 mL
1/4 tsp.	cinnamon	1 mL
1/2 tbsp.	cornstarch	7 mL
1 cup	water	250 mL

Favourite Pastry (see recipe on following page)

- Place ground pork in large saucepan.

- Mix salt, pepper, celery salt, garlic, cloves, cinnamon, cornstarch and water together to make a smooth paste. Stir into the ground pork.

- Simmer, covered, for 30 minutes; then, uncover and simmer for 10 minutes.

- Remove the garlic clove and allow the mixture to cool.

- Meanwhile, make enough pastry for a 2-crust 8" (800 mL) pie.

- Line the pie plate with half the pastry. Pour the meat mixture into the pastry-lined pie plate and cover with remaining pastry. Prick in several places to allow steam to escape during baking.

- Bake in a 400° F (200° C) oven for approximately 30 minutes. Reduce the temperature to 325° F (160° C) and bake for another 20 minutes.

- Serve hot. Serves 6.

❧ Favourite Pastry ❧

1 1/2 cups	pastry flour	375 mL
1/2 tsp.	salt	2 mL
1/2 cup	shortening	125 mL
3 heaping tbsp.	butter	45 mL
1/4 cup	cold water	50 mL

- All ingredients must be cold.

- Measure and sift together the pastry flour and salt. Add the shortening and butter and cut into the flour, until mixture resembles meal. Cut in enough water to make a stiff dough. It should not be crumbly, but should stick together.

- *Tip:* The pastry will be better if it is covered at this point and kept in a cold place until the next day before baking.

Makes an 8" (800 mL) two-crust pie.

Turkey Fair Day

Mother and Father watched as the chickens grew fat in the henhouse. The turkeys were kept inside the coup so they wouldn't run around and lose their meat. For once Mother and Father said it looked like it was going to be an especially good year. We lost few fowl to disease, and the hens laid eggs as if they too knew how much our family depended on their output.

Turkey Fair Day was upon us. The day before, chickens were drawn and plucked and trussed up and tied with fresh cord. Turkeys were doomed to the same fate. Butter was put in the presses and wrapped in waxed paper. Mother worked long into the night making sticky buns so they would be fresh when we loaded the big flat-bottom sleigh the next morning. There was barely room for us five children by the time the fowl was laid out in neat rows, covered with a clean flour-bag sheet and then with heavy blankets to prevent everything from freezing.

We had left the farm before it was barely daylight. Location, according to Mother and Father, could mean the difference between a good day and a bad one. When we found a spot, we children were allowed to come and go as we pleased, but I tended to stay close to the sleigh, excited by the people who walked the main street looking over what the farmers had to offer. And when someone bought something, I could hardly contain myself, I was so pleased.

Father spent a lot of the time visiting other farmers and dropping into Thacker's garage where many of the men met to smoke their pipes and talk about the state of the country. I saw him come back a few times and lift out a turkey and then a big fat chicken, and I was ecstatic to know that he had made a sale away from the sleigh.

14

Mother talked to some of the women from the town, and they all had the same story. The Depression was a terrible worry, and everyone wondered if we could all survive another year. I noticed some of the women with little children and they wore the same worried look I often saw on my mother's face. And then I would see Mother reach under the blanket and lift out a chicken or some eggs or a pound of butter. She would wrap everything in old copies of the *Renfrew Mercury*, and I was only vaguely aware that no money changed hands. And it would look like the woman was about to cry, and I would hear her thank Mother over and over again.

Every farmer's hope was that everything on the sleigh would be sold. And we would pray that it would all sell by late afternoon, because once it got dark, there was no hope of getting rid of the rest of the load. And so I got to counting the number of chickens and turkeys that were left. I would look at the hands on the big clock in the centre of town, and I would say a silent prayer that there would be enough people around to rid us of our fowl, eggs, butter and buns.

Just as I saw the first fingers of the late sun touch down in the west sky, I saw Mother scoop up the last of the few chickens and go off to the building that served as the jail. I wondered if the town had ordered the fowl in advance. And then the sleigh was empty. My sister Audrey folded the blankets and the sheet, and we climbed on board and waited for the long trip home to begin.

When we pulled out of town it was getting dark, and Father lit the wind lantern and hung it on the hook on the front seat of the sleigh…not for light, but to alert other travelers that we were on the road. I sat between Mother and Father and snuggled down under the heavy fur blanket, and thought what a good day it had been. I said to Mother, "Isn't it wonderful that everything sold…weren't we lucky?" Audrey, who was riding with her back against the seat for support, said, "Not everything sold." But it was gone wasn't it? There was nothing left on the sleigh. Mother and Father said not a word of denial, and so Audrey filled in the blanks. "You silly ninny…Mother and Father gave a lot of it away. Didn't you know that?" Mother told Audrey to hush up. And then she said that we had had a good year on the farm. We had no debts and full bellies. We were luckier than most people and sharing was what the Christmas season was all about. Father, who couldn't carry a tune in a hamper, started to sing. And soon we were all caroling to the moonlit fields around us, with the North Star above us, like a beacon leading us home.

☙ Turkey Barley Soup ☙

Mother never wasted a thing back in the 1930s. Soup bones simmered on the back of the Findlay Oval almost constantly, as we always had leftover ham bones, beef ribs from the Sunday roast and, of course, at Christmas time, there was always the turkey carcass. This special turkey barley soup was a favourite, and I still make it today with very few variations from those days on the farm when it was a real stick-to-the-ribs meal. Mother served it with thick slices of homemade bread, and for dessert we had Christmas cookies or cake. It was a full dinner, always served at noon hour...suppers were at night!

1	turkey carcass	1
6 quarts	water	7L
12	peppercorns (or several good shakes from the pepper shaker)	12
2 cups	celery, cut into fairly large pieces	500 mL
3	bay leaves	3
1 large	cooking onion, cut into chunks	1 large
2	garlic cloves, finely chopped	2
1 cup	barley	250 mL
2-28 oz. cans	stewed tomatoes, drained and chopped	2-796 mL cans
1	onion (yes, another one), this time finely chopped	1
1 cup	celery (again, additional), chopped	250 mL
1 cup	carrots, finely chopped	250 mL
2 tsp.	salt	10 mL

- Combine the first seven ingredients in a big pot. Bring to a boil, covered. Turn down the heat and let everything simmer for 1 1/2 hours.

- Remove the carcass and pick the meat off the bones. Store meat in fridge.

- Drain the broth through a sieve into a large bowl. Refrigerate overnight.

- The next day skim off and discard any fat from turkey broth.

- Bring broth back to boil. Add the barley, turkey pieces, tomatoes and remaining ingredients. Cook for at least 45 minutes on reduced heat.

❧ Pea Soup ❧

2 cups	yellow split peas	500 mL
1	ham bone	1
2	large onions	2
4	large carrots, grated	4
2-19 oz. cans	hominy corn	1.1 kg
	salt and pepper to taste	
	butter	

- Soak peas overnight.

- Boil ham bone for several hours in enough water to cover.

- Leaving bone in broth, add the peas—water and all—to the pot, and add extra water if required to cover the bone well.

- Add onions and carrots; simmer 3 hours.

- With a slotted spoon, carefully remove all bone pieces.

- Add the corn, including water.

- Simmer another 30 minutes, adding salt and pepper to taste.

- Serve with a daub of butter in each bowl, if desired.

Serves 10.

Note: This soup will separate with a clear broth on top and a thick mixture settling on the bottom. Simply stir thoroughly before serving.

Letters from School

Miss Crosby of the Northcote School decided early in December that we would all write letters to Santa and send them off to the *Ottawa Farm Journal* where, three times a week, the best were chosen for publication. She thought the exercise would be a good lesson in penmanship, on which she placed great emphasis, and at the same time would teach the value of good citizenship, because as well as telling Santa what we wanted to find under the tree on Christmas morning, we were also ordered to write about what we would do to better our country and the community we lived in.

Marguerite, that bane of my existence at the Northcote School, hadn't been so excited since she was chosen to present a bouquet of flowers to the wife of the Chairman of the Board of Education at the box social that summer. She was absolutely positive her letter would be chosen for publication. Miss Crosby told us that we would each be required to read our letters to the school before she mailed them off in a big brown envelope to the *Ottawa Farm Journal*.

I decided to ask for my usual doll, only this time I asked that it have new clothes on it, not clothes that had been made out of the same material as my pyjamas and my pinnies. Since there wasn't much chance that I'd be getting my wish, I also asked for a new book bag and a diary with a lock and key. We all had diaries at home, since Mother insisted we write down our daily thoughts just after we finished our homework at night, but we used small, five-cent scribblers. The kind of diary I wanted was a little satin-covered book with a clasp lock and a gold key. I even told Santa I would be much obliged if the cover could be blue taffeta, like one I'd seen in the dime store in Renfrew. I had absolutely no problem at all writing what I wished Santa would do for our country. I wished he would get rid of the Depression. I had no idea how he was going to accomplish this, I would leave that up to his powers of magic, but I wrote at great length about all the things I knew about the Depression that I had over-heard my parents talk about downstairs in the kitchen after I had gone to bed. I figured that if I could eliminate those worries for them, I would be benefiting all of Renfrew County.

When it came time to read our letters out to the whole school, I found that most of us had asked for the same wish, that is all except Marguerite. She wished for a new schoolhouse, one with running water and a flush toilet like she had at her house. She just had to throw that in, I suppose, since she constantly talked about how well-off her family was and that her house was one of the few in the entire township that boasted an inside bathroom. The letters were pushed into the big brown envelope, and Miss Crosby said that she would mail it at Briscoe's store on the way home and that she was sure one or two would be picked to run in the *Ottawa Farm Journal.*

We watched the paper like hawks. There were letters from children in Ottawa and Renfrew and a place called Prescott, which we'd never heard of. We'd just about given up hope when Miss Crosby came into school one day with the *Ottawa Farm Journal* folded under her arm. She told us that three of our letters had been chosen for the Santa Claus page. Then she opened up the paper on her desk, and we were told to form a line and come up two at a time to read the letters.

Being in junior grade, I was one of the first, and you can imagine my excitement when I saw my name at the bottom of a letter. Right beside mine was Marguerite's. Our ages, seven years old, where in brackets underneath, but to my absolute horror, through some fluke of the presses, my name appeared under Marguerite's letter and hers under mine. There was my name asking for an inside bathroom for the

Northcote School and raving on about the one we have at home. Marguerite was just as upset to be asking Santa for something as silly as a blue taffeta diary.

I'd like to say that Santa Claus was able to sort the whole thing out at Christmas, but Marguerite did not get a new schoolhouse with an inside privy, and I did not get a taffeta-bound diary. And, as everyone knows, Santa did little to eliminate the ravages of the Depression, which was with us for some time after that letter appeared in the *Ottawa Farm Journal*.

Aunt Lizzie's Christmas Box

We always knew when a hand-me-down box had arrived at the Renfrew station. The ticket agent would telephone and say, "It's here, it's here." And we always knew it was the hand-me-down box from Aunt Lizzie in Regina. Everyone would get in a real tizzy until Father got the horses and sleigh out and headed into town to bring the big wooden box with the aluminum lining back to the farm. For the life of me I can't imagine why Audrey and I anticipated the box…there was never anything in it but boys' clothes.

But that December in the 1930s, we weren't expecting the box. It usually came in late fall or late spring. Yet the call came just a couple of weeks before Christmas, and Audrey said she expected it was because Aunt Lizzie had decided to take pity on us and send each of us a Christmas present in with the second-hand clothes.

That caused great excitement as we all tried to guess what would be in the box. I could hardly stand the anticipation as Father hitched up the horses to the flat-bottom sleigh and headed out for Renfrew with my brother Everett to give him a hand.

It was a Saturday, and goodness knows there was enough to keep us all busy for the day. But the time dragged on, and it was almost dark when we saw Father coming in the long lane off the Northcote Side Road. Emerson and Earl threw on their heavy coats and gum rubbers and headed for the door to help them carry the big box into the kitchen. Mother announced that it wouldn't be touched until after supper and only when the kitchen had been redded up and the floor swept. This only fueled our anticipation.

Finally, Everett was sent out to fetch the crowbar. As we all stood around filled with excitement, he began to pry off the wooden lid. What could be inside? Audrey said the last time Aunt Lizzie visited from Regina she promised her a gold locket…one that had belonged to our grandmother. Audrey mused that it would be nice if this was the time Aunt Lizzie had decided to send it on.

As far as I was concerned, I just *knew* a china doll was tucked inside…down deep amongst all our boy cousins' clothes.

Audrey said she doubted we would see the presents anyway…she was sure Aunt Lizzie would have wrapped them up in Christmas paper and we wouldn't be able to open them until Christmas morning anyway. For some reason that only added to the anticipation.

On the top were the usual Regina newspapers, spread out over everything. Emerson clawed at them and unveiled a pair of brown tweed breeks with a matching jacket. He laid claim to the suit before anyone else had a chance. Then there were layers of other boys' clothes.

There were boys shoes…ugly brown brogues…just like the ones I was wearing…also a gift from Aunt Lizzie in a previous hand-me-down box. And what was that? A silk dress…Audrey ripped it out of the box, but alas it was an old man's kimono…not worth a hoot on a Renfrew County farm. It was tossed aside. There were plaid shirts, more heavy pants for the boys…and then more newspapers from Regina separating these items from what was on the bottom.

I said it was just like Aunt Lizzie to tease us like that and put our presents on the bottom of the box. Everett, half inside, reached down deeper and deeper as piece after piece of boys' clothing came out.

Finally he straightened up. "That's it," he said. We could see the bottom…and could see a few bits of green tea that had once been in the box before it became a container for transporting used clothes to poor cousins at the other end of the country. I was stricken. No Christmas presents. Not even a card. Nothing but boys' clothes and boys' shoes and Regina newspapers.

Mother could see what a disappointment it was, but she wasn't about to hand out sympathy and start a flood of tears. She said how grateful we were to Aunt Lizzie and that she was sure there were some suit-coats there that could be made into skirts for Audrey and me. My bottom lip started to tremble. I was so sure there would be Christmas presents for all of us. Mother once again told us how every disappointment was a character builder. I can only say that during the 1930s I had enough character builders to last me to the turn of the next century.

☙ Acorn Squash ❧

1	acorn squash	1
2	cloves garlic	2
	bacon strips	
1 tsp.	butter	5 mL
	salt	

- Halve each squash and scoop out seeds. Cut a small slit at the end of each half and imbed 1 garlic clove. Line each half with bacon strips.

- Bake on a cookie sheet for approximately 1 hour at 350° F (180° C), until fork-tender.

- Drain bacon drippings off and discard garlic cloves. Cut bacon into small pieces.

- With a fork, blend bacon, butter and salt into each squash half, leaving shells intact. Serve in the shells, piping hot.

Serves 2.

✿ Baked Parsnips ✿

one egg
parsnip, cut in strips
fine breadcrumbs
salt and pepper to taste

- Beat egg until bubbly.

- Dip raw parsnip strips into the egg, then into the breadcrumbs seasoned with salt and pepper.

- Bake at 350° F (180° C) on a cookie sheet until tender, approximately 1 hour.

- *Note*: one egg, as above, will do several parsnips.

❦ Sweet Potato Bake ❦

1 1/2 lbs.	cooked, well-drained sweet potatoes	675 g
	or	
2-14 oz. cans	sweet potatoes, well-drained	2-398 mL cans
1/3 cup	brown sugar	75 mL
1/3 cup	table cream	75 mL
	salt, to taste	
1/2 cup	butter	125 mL
3 tbsp.	white sugar	45 mL
4	slices of pineapple, cut in half	4

- Arrange potatoes in a greased 2-quart (2 L) casserole. Mix brown sugar, table cream and salt and pour over potatoes.

- Dot with butter and sprinkle with the white sugar.

- Arrange the pineapple in a hit-and-miss fashion throughout the sweet potatoes.

- Cover and bake at 325° F (160° C) for 35 minutes. Remove the cover and bake 10 minutes more before serving.

Christmas Concert

The school was brightly decorated that year. The normally grey walls held all our Christmas drawings. A big spruce tree stood in the front corner, full of popcorn balls and tinsel. Every desk had been scrubbed clean, and the senior boys had wiped the floor and polished the stove. We were all ready for the Christmas concert.

Almost all of Saturday was spent getting our clothes ready for the concert. Mother had to create costumes out of nothing, and once again I was the sheep, when all along I wanted to be the angel. But that part in the nativity scene always fell to Marguerite, which gave me yet another reason to hate her with a passion. It wasn't enough that she had a brand new store-bought dress and new, white, ribbed stockings to wear to the concert, but she had to have the best part in the concert as well. My sister Audrey played Mary, but she did nothing more than kneel by the bed of straw and look pious. The angel had to flit about the stage as if she was there on some heavenly deed; of course, Marguerite was more than up to the task. She spent the best part of her years at the Northcote School flitting about. Nonetheless, I envied her the part of the angel and wished, just once, before I got too old and too big, that Miss Crosby would pick me for the part. My sheep costume was nothing more than a long suit of combination underwear with a white cap and tufts of white curried wool taken directly out of our wool bag and tied here and there on the suit of underwear. There was no doubt everyone had to stretch their imaginations more than a country mile to figure out that I was a sheep, whereas there was no doubt in anyone's mind that hateful Marguerite was, indeed, an angel.

The school was packed as usual that Saturday night, and the old pot-bellied stove was fair thumping. Miss Crosby turned the lamps down low and stood just behind the improvised stage curtain with a flashlight which she beamed right on my sister Audrey. We had all been placed in our exact positions. Marguerite was to flit across the stage, peer onto the mound of hay, look directly into the flashlight beam and smile like an angel. I was to do nothing more than squat on all fours with the donkey (who was Cecil) and my brother Emerson (who was the cow). Miss Crosby had cleverly concealed the greater part of them behind the mound of hay to make up for the lack of proper costuming.

The choir, which was made up of everyone else in the school who wasn't in the nativity scene, was singing "Silent Night" with great meaning in the background. Everyone sighed their approval when Marguerite went into her act. Her golden hair (which I knew for a fact came out of a bottle from Ritz's Drugstore) shone like stars. The choir was supposed to stop after each verse so that the angel could make her profound comments. Marguerite was right in her element, taking much longer than necessary to emphasize her words. Well, Emerson didn't like Marguerite any more than I did, and I could hear him let out heavy sighs from behind my sister Audrey.

Then there was a pause. The choir had halted. Marguerite was swooping down to take a final look into the hay at the big doll which had been covered loosely with a piece of flannelette. You could hear a pin drop when suddenly, out of nowhere, came the loud bleating of a sheep; long *b-a-a* sounds as if a ewe was in fierce pain. Every eye on the stage turned in my direction. Even Audrey, who had been warned that under no circumstances was she to look up from the manger, turned completely around and glared at me. I was vigorously shaking my head to indicate I had done nothing.

Miss Crosby scanned the group with the flashlight. Emerson had his eyes shut and was chewing an imaginary cud, just as Miss Crosby had told him to do. The audience was roaring its approval and then started to clap. Marguerite, by now in tears, fled the stage. One of the Briscoe girls who had a lovely singing voice broke into a Christmas carol and the borrowed cretonne curtain was hastily drawn across the piece of chicken wire that had been put up the day before.

Emerson would never admit to making the bleating sound of a sheep in distress. I knew he had done it. Everyone but Marguerite and Miss Crosby knew he had done it. Of course, Marguerite called me everything under the sun and said I had ruined her performance. For once I didn't object to Emerson's shenanigans. In fact, I was delighted that hateful Marguerite thought I had the courage to upstage her. I think now it was the best Christmas concert I had ever gone to all the time I went to the Northcote School.

Mother Longs
for New York

I anticipated and at the same time dreaded the first snowfall. Snow meant rides on the sleigh and in our cutter with our horse King, a snowman topped with Father's old summer straw hat, and playing a game called "the wagon wheel." But it also meant a change in Mother's mood. Mother had a wonderful easiness about her…and she always said life was meant to be enjoyed. But when the first snow arrived, this view was forgotten for the first few days and she became withdrawn and we skirted her in the house as if we were walking on eggshells.

She would take to ambling over to the kitchen window and pulling the curtain back and peering out as if she was looking for someone or something she had mislaid. She would glance over toward the West Hill and then she would turn to stare out the long lane that led to the Northcote Side Road.

I soon learned not to ask her what she was looking for or why she was so quiet. And it was my older sister Audrey who told me one day not to intrude on Mother's reverie, that sooner or later she would come around.

I watch my mother. Ever careful not to intrude. And I take to wondering if I've done something wrong to cause this mood. I ponder my behaviour over the last few days. I didn't have to be reminded to set the supper table, I brought the wood in from the shed to the woodbox, and I never forgot to wear my white pinny over my clothes when I was working in the kitchen. Try as I might I can't think of one solitary thing I've done wrong.

And that was when I would go to my sister Audrey, so much older and so much wiser, and I would ask why Mother seemed to be a million miles away. At first Audrey said it was nothing. But I knew better. After all I was seven years old. I wasn't some ninny from the Barr Line. I knew there was something that was bothering Mother.

And then Audrey took me up to the back bedroom…far away from the stairwell so that she could talk to me in private, and Mother wouldn't hear us from her spot in the kitchen. And even then Audrey would whisper, and I felt as if I was part of some mysterious circumstance.

"She's lonesome," Audrey would say. "But why?" I wanted to know. Weren't we all there…right in the house…how could she be lonesome?

"Because this is the time of year she misses New York City the most," Audrey would say by way of explanation. And she would crane her neck to make sure no one was listening on the stairs. And she would tell me that in the winter the Broadway plays would begin, and the opera and all the things that Mother loved and had left behind were far, far away. Audrey said that when the first snow came, Mother knew that it would just be a matter of time until the farm would be closed in…locked inside a white prison from which there was no chance of escape.

I reminded Audrey that we still went into Renfrew in the winter. Granted it took a little longer with the horses and cutter than it did in the old car. But once or twice a month at least we traveled the Northcote Side Road into town. And sometimes we even got into the O'Brien Theatre when there was egg money left over. Wasn't that enough? And Audrey would say no, that she guessed it wasn't.

And so we would watch and wait. Anticipating the move that would take Mother back to who she was before that first snowfall. Happily that first snow would never last. It would come and go and all that would remain would be the frozen stubble of the front yard. And just as quickly Mother would come out of her dream. It was almost as if that spell had never happened. She would give a great sigh and let the curtain drop back into place and turn from the window. And her face was as it had been before that first snow. Then, like as not, she would clap her hands and order me out to the shed for a bowl of sauerkraut, and send Audrey scurrying to the root cellar for carrots. And she might say, "I feel like bread pudding tonight," and she'd slam around in the cupboard looking for the right pan…and once again, everything would be right with our world.

☙ Sauerkraut ☙

Making sauerkraut was a family affair. We would do perhaps thirty or forty head of cabbage, so that we had a good supply of sauerkraut to tide us over the winter. One of us washed out the big barrel and rolled it into the kitchen. Someone firmly held the cabbage shredder which was like a two-foot-long, three-sided shallow box with a blade in the bottom of it. In the meantime, two of us handed the trimmed cabbage heads to our father, and he shoved them over the blade, and the shredded cabbage fell into the barrel.

35

When the barrel was almost full, coarse salt was sprinkled over the cabbage, and a heavy, washed stone placed on the top. In a day or so, the cabbage formed its own juices, fermented, and magically turned into sauerkraut. The exercise took place late in the fall, so that when we finally rolled the barrel of sauerkraut out of the kitchen into the back shed, its contents soon froze solidly. When we wanted sauerkraut for a meal, we went out with a porcelain pan and an ice pick and chopped away until we had as much as we wanted.

Mother had a delicious way of preparing sauerkraut. It was rinsed once, put in a large frying pan and sautéed with unsalted butter and lots of pepper. We all loved it.

Christmas Shopping

We were always revising our Christmas lists until the writing was almost illegible. This was not the list to Santa. This was for the exchange between siblings. Our gifts to each other might be nothing more than a hanky or a package of gum, but Christmas wouldn't be the same if we didn't have something under the tree for each other. Unfortunately, making suggestions often resulted in a heated argument. This sent Mother into a long discussion on the true meaning of Christmas, which I have to admit was completely lost on squabbling children.

The night in December during the 1930s that I remember the most vividly we were sitting around the kitchen table, and the arguing had reached a fevered pitch. I asked someone to please get me a little miniature Chinese Checkers game. Earl insisted he had asked for the same thing long before I did. He produced his list to prove it. Audrey wanted perfume that did not smell like Miss Crosby at the Northcote School. I said I wanted the same thing. And so it went. Finally Mother slapped down her book on the table. "Enough of this arguing!" she roared. "Every one of you will get a quarter on Saturday. You will all go into Renfrew with your father and me and you will buy your own Christmas gift for yourself, then there will be no more scrapping. You will get exactly what you want. The arguing is over. Now off to bed with the lot of you!"

Upstairs we all thought it was a splendid idea. A whole quarter to buy exactly what we wanted for ourselves. We never felt so rich. So what did it matter if we didn't exchange gifts with each other. We'd have what we wished for from our own lists. We fell asleep dreaming of the hours ahead in the dime store in Renfrew.

When we got into town on Saturday we scattered like chickens in the only store that offered items we could buy for a nickel or a dime. I headed right for the games where the little boxes of Chinese Checkers were on the counter priced at a nickel. I thought of Earl—how he wanted them. Maybe I'd surprise him. I'd still have twenty cents left for myself.

Then I saw the rubber pucks. How Everett wanted a real puck to play shinny on the Bonnechere. It too was a nickel. Then I saw the perfume—big bottles with ribbons around their necks—but they were a dime. I had extra pennies tied in the corner of my hanky, pennies I had been saving for a long time. I thought of my sister Audrey. How she read to me at night, and how she would tie my long, red hair up in rags to make ringlets. I bought the perfume in the green bottle.

Emerson loved licorice pipes. He was pretty hateful to me sometimes, but he was still my brother I reasoned. A nickel got me a whole handful. I caught glimpses of my sister and brothers, but they seemed intent on their own shopping. I still hadn't bought anything for myself as I headed back to the sleigh tied up at Thacker's Garage.

Not much was said all the way back to the farm. We were wrapped up in the fur robes with our parcels clutched to our chests. The brothers unloaded the week's supplies from the sleigh, never for a second letting go of their own bags.

"Well, how did you do?" Mother asked, as she put the supplies away. "Fine," we all answered in unison. "Well, let's see what you bought for yourselves. Come along, Audrey, you show us first. Did you get your perfume?" "Well, uh, no," Audrey said with her eyes downcast. It was soon apparent that not one of us had bought what we wanted on our own lists. No one would show their parcels.

Emerson made a grab for my bags when I slapped him good and hard. We were soon laughing as we faked a tug-of-war for each other's purchases. Mother pulled a chair up to the table. "You didn't buy anything for yourselves, did you?" We all shook our heads. I could see Mother's eyes mist over. She suggested we all have hot cocoa to warm up after the long, cold ride home from Renfrew.

Audrey said she was going to put her parcels under the bed and no one had better dare look. The rest of us followed suit. When we returned to the kitchen Mother had steaming hot cups of cocoa on the table as she always did when she was particularly pleased with us. She ruffled our hair and squeezed the backs of our necks as we all took our places around the old pine table.

Jail

It was always at Christmas time that Mother would get the urge to do something splendid for someone else. And every year, it seems now, Mother had a different cause she felt compelled to work for.

Like the year she decided to do something for all those poor "unfortunates," as she called them, who found themselves ensconced in the county jail. Father said they were there of their own accord. Mother said they were there because their lot in life was such that they had no control over it. Father just chewed on his pipe and muttered something in German.

But once Mother got an idea into her head, there was little he or anyone else could do to shake it free. And so she set about to make sure the inmates of the county jail would not be forgotten on Christmas Day. The first thing she did was go off to Renfrew to check with the authorities to see if there was, in fact, anyone in jail. She found out that there were several "unfortunates." Then she went off to the Salvation Army to see if one night close to Christmas they would sing under the jailhouse window. They seemed pleased with the idea of having a purpose for their street performances and willingly agreed, especially when Mother offered up her five children as singers, as well.

And then she had to get permission to take in a meal. This proved to be a little more difficult. Emerson said everything she took in would have to be gone over with a fine-tooth comb, as the police would be sure to suspect her of burying a file in the potatoes. Mother paused in her plan to weigh what Emerson had said. Especially when Emerson added that he wouldn't be at all surprised if she ended up in jail with the inmates.

My sister Audrey and I, who weren't at all pleased with the idea in the first place, begged Mother to change her mind, but we had no more success than did Father. She was going to take some Christmas food into the jail and that's all there was to it. Now, what to take in was the problem. It meant another meeting in Renfrew, and by then Father was so riled up over the idea that no one dared mention the word "jail" in front of him. And, of course, he wouldn't budge off the farm for the trip into town for a stop at the county jail. So on a cold December Saturday, Mother, Audrey and I bundled up and headed into Renfrew in the cutter. Audrey and I waited outside while Mother went in to make her inquiries. She was gone the longest while, and when she came out she was red in the face and muttering to herself.

It was a fast trip home, with Mother saying hardly a word. When we fell into the kitchen, half-frozen and hungry from the all-day trip into town, Father was settled comfortably in the rocking chair. The last thing he wanted to hear about were tales of "the gangsters," as *he* called the inmates at the county jail. But Mother could contain herself no longer. She wasn't allowed to take in a Christmas dinner, and that was the short and the long of it. She was, however, allowed to take in a "treat" the week before Christmas. Emerson wanted to know if that meant a store-bought present. This comment caused Father to stir long enough to say, "It does not." Mother said she would make her famous Boston baked beans. Everyone loved her beans, she said.

The beans simmered all day and baked all night in the old Findlay Oval. The next day the aroma floated up the staircase when we got out of bed in the morning. This was the day they would be taken into Renfrew. And yes, Audrey and I were going to be allowed to go with Mother. And maybe we would be given permission to go into the jail, as well.

It was a cold, blustery day when we set out for Renfrew. The beans were in a big roasting pan sitting on a half-dozen oven-heated bricks, wrapped in thick newspaper and then in a few layers of quilts. We got to the jail around noon hour, and I had never been inside such a building before. By this time the inmates were well-acquainted with my mother. One of them yelled, "Hello, Mabel." The woman who fed them was right there to take the roaster, and when she unwrapped the coverings, she said in a booming voice, "Beans…isn't that lovely." Groans could be heard from the few inmates. "Beans. We've had beans every day since we've been in here. Did you say beans?"

I wondered if there might be a riot. Audrey said not to be silly…three people couldn't cause a riot. We drove home in the cutter, and we were all the way to Briscoe's General Store before Mother spoke. She said she didn't see any need to tell Father about the reception we had had at the county jail. And then she perked right up…"Besides," she said, her old self again, "it's the thought that counts."

✲ Jailhouse (Boston baked) Beans ✲

My mother used a large roasting pan when she made these beans, for church suppers or jail visits! This recipe feeds 12 easily—just halve the amounts if you want a smaller batch.

4 cups	white beans	1L
1/2 lb.	fat salt pork	225 g
1 cup	chopped onion	250 mL
2 tsp.	salt	10 mL
	mixed with	
3/4 cup	molasses	175 mL
1 tbsp.	dry mustard	15 mL
2 tbsp	brown sugar	30 mL

• Wash the beans, discarding dark ones.

• Cover with cold water and soak overnight.

• Drain the next morning, and again cover with cold water; cook very slowly until the skins begin to burst (approximately 1 hour).

• Drain, saving the cooking water.

• Place onion and a slice of the salt pork in the bottom of a 4-quart (4 L) roasting pan or casserole, and add the beans.

• Bring bean water to a boil and add 1 cup (250 mL) of it to salt, molasses, mustard and brown sugar mixture. Mix well and pour over the beans. Add enough water to cover beans.

- Slice through the salt port rind, but do not sever remaining pork. Place the whole piece of salt pork down into the beans in the centre of dish, leaving only the rind portion exposed.

- Cover the pot and bake for at least 6 hours at 300° F (150° C).

- Add water as needed; beans should always be moist.

- Remove cover for the last 45 minutes to crisp the rind.

Christmas Baking

The aromas alone would tell you, when walking into any kitchen in the Ottawa Valley back in the 1930s, that Christmas was just a spit away. Early in December the Christmas baking began, and my mother, who was French Canadian, made all her favourite dishes first, and then when she was sure they were safely out of the way, she would help my father (who was German) make some of the things that were traditional to his family.

When the Christmas baking began, every child was pressed into service. The youngest greased cake pans, cut cookies and peeled apples, while the older children were allowed more difficult jobs like creaming butter and sugar, making icings and separating eggs. All of us wore large flour-bag aprons which covered us from our chins to our toes. The baking was done in the evening or on Saturday so we children could be part of the festivities. I can remember our mother making the job into a kind of party, so that the memories I have now of those pre-Christmas baking sessions are memories of good times and laughter and a feeling of cosy warmth that only partly came from the heat of the Findlay Oval.

My mother had many specialties, and one of them has become a tradition in my family as well. They were the French tourtières. Father would say, "They're just plain pork pies to me. You can call them whatever foreign name you like, but they're pork pies, plain and simple." Mother would ignore him, as she simmered the lean ground pork with a garlic clove and a pinch of cinnamon and ground cloves. This was piled into rich pastry crusts and wrapped tightly and tied with string. They were then put out into the summer kitchen to freeze solid, and as they were needed, they were brought in and baked in the oven. My father insisted they would taste better if they had a layer of mashed potatoes between the meat mixture and the crust. "That's the way the Germans make pork pies," he'd insist.

It seemed to be a contest between my mother and father to see who could come up with the most delicacies for the holiday season. Father's specialties were much more stable, and as mother would say, "You'd need a cast-iron stomach for some of those German concoctions." The sauerkraut and the salt pork barrels would already be filled and out in the back kitchen, and from the sandbin in the cellar, Father would bring up carrots which were cut into long strips and "done down," as he called it, with vinegar and salt and brown sugar. These delicious carrot pickles were a special treat to us, but Mother insisted carrots were best used in a stew or mashed with a turnip.

45

Father also made wonderful cabbage rolls for Christmas, and these were packed in a big crock and put out in the well-stocked storeroom at the back of the house. By the time all the French dishes were made and all the German dishes, the little lean-to looked like the pantry of one of the country's wealthiest families. And when we looked at the array of Christmas treats, we never once thought of the Depression. Most of the ingredients were things which were readily available on the farm. Rich cream, fresh daily. Golden butter made in our own churn. Garlic buds taken from the strip of cloves hanging in the kitchen. Vegetables from the cellar bin and honey from our own bees. Any wonder we children never gave any thought to the state of the country's economy?

Then all through the Christmas season our farm neighbours would drop in for a visit and we would rush out to the summer kitchen when we saw their sleigh rounding the corner at the barn. By the time the porcelain kettle was boiling on the front of the stove, the shortbread would be thawed out for eating. There was a bond between the country folk, held together by the simplest of ties—friendship, caring and the feeling of belonging to a close community. The bonds were there all year round, but at Christmas time we were all especially aware of the preciousness of those Valley neighbours.

✥ Old-Fashioned Christmas Fruitcake ✥

1/2 cup	shortening	125 mL
3/4 tsp.	salt	3 mL
1/2 tsp.	each of cinnamon, clove, nutmeg and allspice	2 mL
2 tbsp.	cocoa	30 mL
1 3/4 cup	white sugar	425 mL
3	eggs	3
1 1/2 tsp.	baking soda	7 mL
2 cups	twice-sifted flour	500 mL
1 cup	finely chopped dates	250 mL
1/2 cup	dark raisins, soaked overnight	125 mL
3/4 cup	chopped nuts (pecans or walnuts, as preferred)	175 mL
1 1/2 cup	canned applesauce	375 mL

- Grease and flour a 10" tube pan. Preheat oven to 350° F (180° C).

- In large mixer bowl, blend shortening, salt, spices and cocoa. Add sugar and cream well. Add eggs, one at a time. Beat well after each addition.

- Mix baking soda with flour, sprinkle fruit and nuts with 2 tbsp. (30 mL)of the flour.

- Add remaining flour to batter alternately with applesauce.

- Fold in fruit and nuts.

- Pour into pan and bake an hour (or until a metal skewer comes out clean). Do not overcook.

- Frost with your favourite icing. (We like a plain white, butter icing, although Mother often used almond paste.)

❧ Eggnog Bread ❧

This is a wonderful treat to keep on hand for unexpected company. It's easy to make and freezes well.

2 3/4 cups	flour	675 mL
3/4 cup	sugar	175 mL
2 tbsp.	baking powder	30 mL
1 tsp.	salt	5 mL
1/2 tsp.	mace	2 mL
1 1/2 cups	eggnog	375 mL
1/4 cup	butter, melted	50 mL
1	egg, beaten	1
2 tbsp.	rum	30 mL
3/4 cup	chopped pecans	175 mL
3/4 cup	mixed candied fruit	175 mL

49

- Preheat oven to 350° F (180° C).

- Grease a loaf pan (I use my meatloaf pan).

- In large bowl, use spoon to mix first 5 ingredients.

- Stir in the eggnog, butter, egg and rum. Don't overstir…stir just until everything is moistened. (It will be lumpy.)

- Fold in the nuts and fruit.

- Spread mixture in pan and bake for approximately 1 hour. Use a skewer to test for doneness. Do not overcook.

- Cool the bread on a wire rack, leaving it in the pan for about 10 minutes. Remove from pan and cool. Wrap and freeze.

This keeps for 3 to 4 months. To serve, thaw for approximately 4 hours, unwrapped, at room temperature.

☙ Cherry Drops ❧

1 1/2 cups	sifted icing sugar	375 mL
1/2 cup	butter	125 mL
1 1/2 cups	coconut	375 mL
	graham wafers, crushed	
48	maraschino cherries	48

- Mix first 3 ingredients together and shape into small balls.

- Place a cherry in the centre of each ball, then roll in crushed graham wafers.

- Chill and store in refrigerator.

Makes approximately 4 dozen cookies.

❧ Butterscotch Log ❧

1-6 oz. pkg.	butterscotch chips	170 g
1/3 cup	sweetened condensed milk	75 mL
1/2 tsp.	vanilla	2 mL
1/3 cup	pecans, chopped	75 mL
1	egg white, slightly beaten	1
	pecan halves	

- Melt the butterscotch over hot (not boiling) water.

- Remove from heat and stir in milk and vanilla. Add nuts and mix well.

- Chill mixture until firm enough to handle.

- Form into a roll and wrap in wax paper. Unwrap and scrape the surface with the tines of a fork. Brush the roll with egg white.

- Press pecan halves into the roll at 1/2" (1 cm) intervals to cover the surface.

- Wrap again in wax paper and chill.

- Cut into 1/2" (1 cm) slices.

Makes approximately 2 dozen cookies.

✥ Brown Sugar Cookies ✥

1 cup	shortening	250 mL
2 cups	brown sugar	500 mL
2	eggs	2
1/2 cup	sour milk*	125 mL
3 1/2 cups	flour	875 mL
1 tsp.	baking soda	5 mL
1 tsp.	salt	5 mL

53

* add 1 to 1 1/2 tbsp. (15 to 22 mL) of vinegar to milk to sour it.

• Mix together well the shortening, brown sugar, and eggs. Stir in the sour milk.

• Sift together flour, baking soda and salt and add to the sugar mixture.

• Drop by rounded teaspoonsful onto a greased cookie sheet.

• Bake at 400° F (200° C) for 8-10 minutes. Remove immediately from baking sheet.

Makes approximately 6 dozen cookies.

☺ Gumdrop Cookies ☺

1/2 cup	shortening	125 mL
1/2 cup	brown sugar	125 mL
1/2 cup	white sugar	125 mL
1	egg	1
1 cup	rolled oats	250 mL
1 cup	corn flakes	250 mL
1 cup	flour	250 mL
1/2 tsp.	salt	2mL
1/2 tsp.	baking soda	2mL
1 tsp.	baking powder	5 mL
1/2 cup	coconut	125 mL
1/2 cup	gumdrops, cut into small pieces	125 mL

- Mix all ingredients together in a large bowl. Drop by rounded teaspoonsful onto a greased cookie sheet.

- Bake at 350° F (180° C) for 15 minutes.

Makes 4 1/2 to 5 dozen cookies.

☙ Ginger Cookies ❧

1 cup	white sugar	250 mL
1	egg	1
2/3 cups	cooking oil	150 mL
1/4 cup	molasses	50 mL
2 cups	all-purpose flour	500 mL
1 tsp.	baking soda	5 mL
1 tsp.	cinnamon	5 mL
1/2 tsp.	ginger	2 mL
1/2 tsp.	ground mixed spices	2 mL
1/4 cup	white sugar	50 mL

55

- Beat the sugar and egg together until fluffy. Add the oil and molasses.

- Sift the flour, baking soda, cinnamon, ginger and mixed spices together and add to egg mixture.

- Shape into 1" (3 cm) balls and dip in the sugar. Flatten balls and bake on a greased cookie sheet at 350° F (180° C) for 10 minutes. Remove immediately.

Makes approximately 2 1/2 dozen cookies.

☙ Molasses Cookies ☙

1/2 cup	butter	125 mL
1/2 cup	white sugar	125 mL
3/4 cup	molasses	175 mL
1	egg	1
2 1/2 cups	flour	625 mL
1 1/2 tsp.	ginger	7 mL
1 tsp.	cinnamon	5 mL
1/4 tsp.	salt	1 mL
2 tbsp.	baking soda	30 mL
1/4 cup	water	50 mL

- Cream together butter and sugar. Add molasses and egg to the creamed mixture.

- Sift together flour, ginger, cinnamon and salt, and add to creamed mixture.

- Dissolve baking soda in water and add to mixture.

- Roll out and cut with cookie cutters.

- Bake at 400° F (200° C) for 10 minutes.

Makes approximately 4 dozen cookies.

✣ Pecan Snowballs ✣

1 cup	pastry flour	250 mL
1 1/2 tbsp.	sugar	22 mL
8 tbsp.	butter	120 mL
1 tsp.	vanilla	5 mL
1 cup	pecans, chopped	250 mL

- Measure the flour and sift with the sugar.

- Cream butter and add vanilla and pecans, then the flour-sugar mixture.

- Shape dough into 1" (3 cm) balls and place on an ungreased cookie sheet.

- Bake at 300° F (150° C) for 25 to 30 minutes.

- When cooled, roll cookies in sifted icing sugar.

Makes approximately 1 1/2 dozen cookies.

☙ Orange Crisps ☙

3 tbsp.	liquid honey	45 mL
1 tbsp.	boiling water	15 mL
2 tbsp.	grated orange rind	30 mL
1 tbsp.	sherry	15 mL
1/2 cup	butter	125 mL
1 cup	sugar	250 mL
1 1/2 cups	flour	375 mL
1 tbsp.	baking powder	15 mL
1/2 tsp.	salt	2 mL

- Combine honey and boiling water; blend, and stir in orange rind and sherry.

- Cream butter and sugar until fluffy. Add the flour, sifted with the baking powder and salt.

- Stir in the honey mixture, blending well.

- Chill the dough until firm.

- Form into small balls, place on an ungreased cookie sheet and flatten with a fork.

- Bake at 350° F (180° C) for 8 to 10 minutes.

Makes approximately 2 dozen cookies.

December Birthday

When I was little I thought I had been dealt a terrible blow by fate to have been born in the month of December. My little friend Joyce had a summer birthday, and I thought she was the luckiest person alive. Here was my birthday just a couple of weeks away from Christmas, which meant I hadn't a hope of ever having a party, and whatever presents I got always came with the message…"It isn't much, but then Christmas is just around the corner."

But on my eighth birthday my Mother said things would be different. She cautioned that the gifts would still be simple, but since my Montreal cousins were here and would be spending the Christmas season with us on the farm, we would be having a little birthday party.

I had never had a birthday party of any description, and so I looked forward to that day with great excitement. The celebration was to be on a Saturday night. That made me feel very grown up indeed, since most Saturday nights were reserved for the adult get-together in the community. And so the Saturday before, there was great whispering and talk behind my back, as my brothers, sister and cousins Ronny and Terry planned what they would buy me with the ten cents each that Mother had allotted them.

We were all to go into Renfrew on the big flat-bottom sleigh, bundled up like bags of feed, sitting back to back and protected by the big, fur blankets. I was to spend the time with Mother while everyone else went off in different directions to secure my birthday gifts. And I wasn't to look after them either, although I chanced a peek from behind my mitten-clad hands and saw Audrey and Emerson head right for the dime store. The others went scurrying down the street, I couldn't fathom where.

I had no idea how I was going to put in the next seven days. The presents were hidden when we got home, and young Terry was threatened with severe mutilation if he as much as breathed a hint of what was bought in Renfrew. Ronny's gift sounded the most exciting. He said I would never guess what it was in a million years and that he went off on his own to buy it, and absolutely no one in the entire family knew what it was or where he had hidden it. He gave me lots of clues, but I couldn't for the life of me figure out what was reddish pink, had skin on it, and was my absolute favourite thing in the whole world.

I already had a new art gum, since Mother had to buy me one when Cecil ate the one I started school with in September. And hair ribbons certainly didn't have skin on them. For the life of me, I couldn't imagine what it was.

Finally Saturday rolled around, and that day our chores seemed to take longer than ever before. Supper dishes were cleared away in jig-time, the oilcloth wiped clean, and Mother said it was time for everyone to go fetch my presents. Even my fingertips tingled. Ronny kept yelling, "Open mine first, open mine first," but little Terry was already tearing the paper of the one he was supposed to be giving me, and so I relieved him of his in a hurry. It was a box of Cracker Jacks. Ronny announced that Terry had only spent a nickel and that he blew the other nickel on an ice-cream cone.

And then Ronny thrust his present under my nose. It was wrapped in brown paper and tied with string, and he had printed his name across the front. It was soft, and Ronny said he bet a nickel I couldn't guess what it was. He was right. I opened the string, remembering how to save it, as I always did to add to the big ball in the cupboard drawer.

And then the parcel was laid open. I could only stare in disbelief. It looked like bologna, but it was bright green around the edges, and the skin had left each slice and was curled into a hard circle. "I know how much you love bologna…and I bought a whole dime's worth," Ronny announced, proudly.

He took a closer look at the unwrapped parcel. "It was all right last Saturday when I bought it. I didn't even unwrap it. It's been under the mattress ever since. What do you think happened to it, Aunty?" he asked Mother. Before she could answer, my three brothers started to laugh. Emerson was holding his sides and rolling on the floor. Mother gave him a swat that straightened him up in a hurry. I told Ronny I thought it was the most wonderful gift I had ever had. That made Terry start to cry, "I thought you liked my Cracker Jacks." Mother was cutting the green edges off the bologna and said a few minutes in the fry pan and it would be right as rain.

61

I no longer remember what the other gifts were. But I know to this day, I never have a piece of bologna that I don't think of that special gift from cousin Ronny.

Church Choir

The Lutheran church always had its Christmas concert early, so as not to interfere with all the festivities going on during the holiday season. There were special prayer meetings, hymn sings and evening services, all held during the month of December, and these events went right up to and included Christmas Eve, and so our enormous, very serious minister always wanted to get the church concert out of the way early.

And when he gave the command that he expected everyone out for rehearsal…he meant everyone! And so it was that on a bitterly cold December night, we five children and the two Lapointe cousins were bundled onto the flat-bottom sleigh and hauled off to the church. The fire in the pot-bellied stove hadn't had enough time to heat the building, and we could see our breath when we went inside. The organist was trying to coax a tune out of the old foot-pedal machine, and everyone was standing around with their coats and mitts on.

The minister had his great cape on over his long robes, and in spite of the bitter cold, beads of sweat were beginning to form on his forehead. That meant one thing…he considered this serious business. We were ordered up to the front of the church where the minister arranged us in order of size. That put my cousin Ronny in the second row, and his young brother Terry standing right beside me.

The organist had picked the carols we were to sing, and she was finally able to get some squawky music out of the organ. It was then that Terry said he was too tired to sing. And he opened his mouth wide and yawned loudly, causing the organist to stop dead in her tracks. The minister said that was nonsense, that he wasn't too tired, and to open his mouth and sing with the rest of us. There was another loud yawn…almost a sigh, and I was afraid Terry was going to keel right over in a heap.

To question this "man of the cloth" was unheard of, and the rest of us stood ramrod straight, waiting for the nod from the organist to begin. Terry was now yawning every time he took a breath, and like an infectious disease, he soon had all of us in the front row yawning right with him. I could hardly keep my eyes open. I had no idea what we were singing, and everything started to drone in my ears. All I wanted to do was lie down and have a sleep.

It wasn't long until the second row had caught the affliction. After all, we were used to being in bed by eight o'clock, and goodness knows what time it was by then, but it seemed to me it was the middle of the night. The minister's face was beet red and wet with perspiration. But still he pressed on with the rehearsal…or what was supposed to pass for a rehearsal. And then I felt Terry's head hit my shoulder. He was perfectly still and, I thought, just resting a bit. I felt the utmost compassion for my young cousin, who couldn't have been any more than five years old.

And then I heard the softest snores…gentle at first…and then a little louder…and all the time we were singing and the organ was playing and the minister was making great sweeping motions with his arms. But little Terry slept on. Standing up, straight as a die, with nothing holding him but my shoulder. Just hearing him snoring softly, made me more sleepy than ever, and I longed for my feather bed. Did the minister have no mercy, I wondered?

And then, as gently as you please, wee Terry folded up like a fan and quietly slipped to the floor, dead to the world. The minister never missed a beat…he was going to finish this rehearsal if every one of us fell asleep. And then the organist caught the yawns. First she tried to hide them, but they soon came in rapid succession. The minister could not ignore the hour any longer, or the distress we were all suffering. He finally called a halt to the practice, and announced that the next rehearsal would be held right after school. It took both my sister Audrey and my brother Everett to carry Terry out to the sleigh. He never opened an eye.

As the minister was locking the door of the church behind us, we heard him discussing with the organist how the young people of the day just didn't seem to have the spark that children had in the olden days. "Not nearly as much energy as we old folks," he added. "You are so right, Reverend," the organist replied, as she stifled a yawn behind a mitten-clad hand.

Christmas Planning

I have neither the time nor the patience to start Christmas planning in December. Over the years I have developed a plan that allows me to enjoy Christmas with my family without the hassle of last-minute cooking, gift buying, card-writing and housecleaning.

After finding that I was never in any of the Christmas morning photos taken when my children were little (I was always out in the kitchen peeling turnips), I now try to put most of my Christmas dinner in the freezer during November. By Christmas morning, all I have to do is stuff the turkey, put it in the oven, and heat the dishes from the freezer. So what if the potatoes are in a cream sauce? So what if instead of mashed turnip, I serve turnip and apple casserole? If it means I have more free time with my family, that's the way it's going to be from now on.

Christmas Menu I

A plan-ahead buffet!

This menu was aired on CBC "Radio Noon" in the early 1980s in an effort to take the last-minute hassle out of preparing and serving a holiday meal. As a result of that show, over 3000 listeners requested copies of this plan-ahead, hassle-free buffet!

Cheese Ball with Crackers
Special Roast Turkey with Hazelnut Dressing and Orange Glaze
Cranberries with a Difference
Moulded Christmas Salad
Moulded Salmon
Potatoes in Rich Cream Sauce
Yams with Pineapple
Asparagus with Pimentos and Red Onions
Tossed Salad with Homemade Croutons
French Fruit Bread
Ricotta Cheese Torte

Step 1   *First week of December*

- Prepare bread crumbs for turkey dressing; freeze in a plastic bag.

- Dice onions; freeze in a plastic bag.

- Roast hazelnuts; freeze.

- Take the above 3 items from the freezer the day before using using and thaw in the refrigerator.

Make croutons for tossed salad . . .

- Melt butter in a large skillet.

- Sprinkle generously with garlic salt.

- Sauté bread cubes until golden.

- Bake at 250° F (120° C) until dry and crisp.

- Store in an airtight jar.

Step 2   *December 9*

Make cranberries and freeze . . .

✑ Cranberries with a Difference ✑

2	oranges	2
1 lb.	cranberries	500 g
2 cups	white sugar	500 mL
3	stalks of celery, diced	3
pinch	ginger	pinch

- Cut unpeeled oranges into large pieces, removing the seeds.

- Put oranges and cranberries through a food grinder or processor. Do not overchop.

- Stir in sugar, celery and pinch of ginger.

- Simmer for a few minutes. Do not boil.

- Taste and adjust the sugar, adding more if necessary.

- Store in a freezer container. Take from the freezer the day before using and thaw in the refrigerator.

Step 3   *December 11*

Make moulded Christmas salad and salmon mould.

❧ Christmas Salad ❧

8 oz.	cream cheese	250 g
1/2 cup	white sugar	125 mL
1 cup	crushed pineapple and juice	250 mL
1 lb.	frozen strawberries, thawed	500 g
1 cup	whipping cream	250 mL
few drops	red food colouring	few drops

- Warm cheese at room temperature until soft.

- Blend in the sugar, mixing thoroughly until the sugar dissolves.

- Add the pineapple and juice and thawed strawberries. Stir well (don't worry about lumps).

- Let stand while whipping cream until stiff. Add a few drops of red food colouring to cream.

- Fold cream into fruit.

- Pour into a favourite mould.

- Freeze (*note*: allow salad to set well first before freezing; this is true for freezing any moulded salad).

- When time to serve, unmould on a salad plate. Before serving you may wish to add finely chopped walnut to the top and/or cut cherries.

❧ Salmon Mould ❧

2 1/2 tbsp.	unflavoured gelatin	37 mL
1/2 tsp.	salt	2 mL
1/4 tsp.	mustard	1 mL
2 tbsp.	sugar	30 mL
1/2 tbsp.	flour	7 mL
1	egg	1
1 cup	milk	250 mL
1/4 cup	vinegar	50 mL
1 tbsp.	butter	15 mL
2 cups	solid canned salmon	500 mL
1 cup	frozen peas	250 mL
3	eggs, hard-cooked and chopped	3

- Soften the gelatin in 4 tbsp. (60 mL) cold water.

- Mix salt, mustard, sugar, flour, one egg, milk, vinegar and butter together in a saucepan.

- Bring to a boil.

- Dissolve the gelatin in the hot dressing, stirring constantly.

- Add the salmon, which you've broken down with a fork.

- Stir well to mix thoroughly.

- Add peas (do not defrost) and hard-cooked, chopped eggs.

- Turn into a lightly greased 2-quart (2 mL) mould.

- Refrigerate until set, wrap well and freeze.

Step 4   *December 16*

Make Ricotta Cheesecake.

❧ Ricotta Cheesecake ❧

This is a spectacular cake with a very different taste. And even though it seems like a lot of fuss, it goes together with little trouble. And the results are worth it. It serves 16 people beautifully.

6	eggs, separated	6
1 1/4 cups	white sugar	300 mL
1 1/4 cups	flour	300 mL
1 tsp.	vanilla	5 mL
pinch	salt	pinch
1 tbsp.	grated orange peel	15 mL
1 1/2 lbs.	ricotta cheese	750 g
1 cup	confectioner's sugar	250 mL
3 cups	heavy whipping cream	750 mL
1 cup	mixed candied fruit	250 mL
1/2 cup	semi-sweet chocolate pieces	125 mL
1/4 cup	orange liqueur	50 mL
1/4 cup	orange juice	50 mL

- Preheat oven to 350° F (180° C).

- In a large mixing bowl, beat egg whites until stiff peaks form. Set aside.

- In a smaller bowl, beat egg yolks with the sugar until thick and lemony.

- Gradually beat in the flour, vanilla and salt until blended. (The mixture will be very thick.)

- With spatula, fold in the orange peel and one-third of the beaten egg whites into the yolk mixture.

- Then fold the yolk mixture into the remaining egg whites.

- Pour batter into an ungreased Springform pan.

- Bake approximately 45 minutes, or until the top springs back when lightly touched. Do not overcook.

- Turn upside down, and cool completely.

Cake can be frozen at this point by removing the cake gently from the pan. Use a knife to loosen the edges of the cake before releasing the spring of the pan. Wrap tightly to seal.

Remove from the freezer the day before serving. Allow to defrost while still wrapped. When almost thawed, remove wrapping and cut the cake in half horizontally. Place one half on a favourite cake plate. Mix liqueur and orange juice. Sprinkle cake half on cake plate with half of the orange juice mixture.

See next page for Filling.

Filling (for Ricotta Cheesecake)

- In a blender or food processor, using the knife blade, blend the ricotta cheese and 3/4 cup (175 mL) of confectioner's sugar until smooth.

- Spoon the mixture into a medium-sized bowl.

- Whip cream (half of the 3 cups called for) until soft peaks form.

- Gently fold the cheese mixture into the beaten cream.

- Reserve 2 tbsp. (30 mL) of the candied fruit, and stir the rest into the cheese mixture.

- Fold in semi-sweet chocolate pieces.

- Place mixture in refrigerator for approximately 20 minutes until firm.

- When firm, spread half of the cheese mixture on the bottom half of the cake on the cake plate. Sprinkle the rest of the orange juice mixture on the remaining cake layer and flip it onto the other half of the cake (cut sides together).

- Top cake with the remainder of the cheese mixture.

- Beat the remaining whipped cream and 1/4 cup (50 mL) of confectioner's sugar until stiff peaks form. Spoon onto cake, covering top and sides.

- Sprinkle the top with the remaining candied fruit.

Once put together, this dessert can be stored in the refrigerator a full day in a large, covered cake tin.

Step 5 *December 18*

Make vegetable casseroles.

☙ Yams with Pineapple ☙

Use canned sweet potatoes. They're easier to handle and they retain their colour. However, you may use fresh ones if you prefer. (If using fresh yams, cook, cool and then pare.)

- Allow about 1/2 yam per serving, and judge the recipe accordingly.

- Place yams in a serving dish that will freeze.

- Cut rings of canned pineapple in half, saving juice. Tuck pineapple rings around the dish at intervals, using a large can of pineapple.

- Mix pineapple juice with:

1 tbsp.	brown sugar	15 mL
1/2 tbsp.	cinnamon	7 mL
1 tbsp.	cornstarch	15 mL

- Blend until smooth.

- Pour over yams and pineapple.

- Wrap and freeze.

- Defrost the day of serving.

- Dot with butter and bake, uncovered, in a 350° F (180° C) oven until the sauce thickens slightly. Occasionally spoon some of the sauce over the potatoes while cooking.

☙ Asparagus with Pimentos and Red Onions ☙

- Use either canned asparagus or cooked, fresh asparagus.

- Drain well, handling the stalks carefully.

- Lay stalks out lengthwise in a flat casserole.

- Using approximately 1/2 cup (125 mL) of chopped pimentos, scatter over the asparagus.

- Gently sauté in butter 1 cup of red onion rings. Do not brown. They should remain firm. Without draining off the butter, place onions on asparagus and pimentos.

- Wrap dish for the freezer.

- Cook 1/2 lb. (250 g) of bacon until crisp. Drain well, cool and then crumble. Wrap and freeze separately.

When ready to serve, thaw both the casserole and bacon. Spread bacon evenly over top of asparagus casserole. Heat thoroughly in oven.

Step 6 *To prepare whenever you wish before Christmas:*
French Fruit Bread with Apricot Glaze and Caraway Cheese Ball.

❦ French Fruit Bread ❦

This loaf serves 12.

4	eggs	4
3/4 cup	white sugar	175 mL
1 1/2 cups	sifted, self-rising flour	375 mL
1 tsp.	cinnamon	5 mL
1/2 tsp.	salt	2 mL
1/2 cup	chopped blanched almonds	125 mL
1/2 cup	chopped blanched hazelnuts	125 mL
1 1/4 cup	light raisins	300 mL
1/4 cup	diced candied lemon peel	50 mL
1 tsp.	lemon juice	5 mL
2 tbsp.	rum	30 mL

Apricot Glaze (recipe on following page)
confectioner's sugar

- Preheat oven to 350° F (180° C).

- Beat eggs and sugar until thick and lemon-coloured.

- Sift flour, cinnamon and salt into a medium bowl. Stir in nuts and fruits.

- Blend lemon juice with rum.

- Add flour mixture to egg mixture, alternately with rum mixture, folding carefully after each addition. Blend well.

- Pour into a well-greased and floured round loaf pan (a regular loaf pan will do). Bake in oven for 45 minutes, or until bread is done.

- Remove to wire rack and cool for 5 minutes. Then remove bread from pan and cool completely.

- Brush top of loaf with Apricot Glaze and sprinkle with confectioner's sugar.

- When cool, wrap tightly and freeze.

❧ Apricot Glaze ❧

1 cup	apricot jam	250 mL
1 1/4 cups	water	300 mL
3/4 cup	fine sugar	175 mL

- Combine all ingredients in a heavy pan and heat until jam is dissolved. Stir constantly.

- Bring to a slow boil, and continue cooking until reduced to about 1 1/2 cups (375 mL). Strain through a sieve.

❧ Caraway Cheese Ball ❧

3 3-oz. pkgs.	cream cheese, softened	255 g
1 4-oz. pkg.	blue cheese, crumbled	115 g
2 tsp.	bourbon	10 mL
3/4 tsp.	dry mustard	3 mL
2 tbsp.	toasted caraway seeds	30 mL

- In a small bowl, with an electric mixer at medium speed, beat cheeses until soft.

- Beat in bourbon and mustard.

- With hands, shape cheese mixture into a ball.

- Wrap and refrigerate if using in a day or two. If not, wrap in buttered wax paper, then into foil and freeze.

- Just before serving, roll ball in sesame seeds.

Step 7 *December 24*

Shred salad greens and store in a plastic bag.
Make Potatoes in Rich Cream Sauce.

✥ Potatoes in Rich Cream Sauce ✥

- Prepare your potatoes for boiling. Cut into large chunks. Cook only until barely tender (potatoes will continue to cook in the reheating on Christmas Day).

- Make a rich cream sauce. Increase the recipe depending on the number of potatoes you plan to use. The following recipe will be sufficient for 6 large potatoes.

3 tbsp.	butter	45 mL
2-3 tbsp.	flour	30-45 mL
1/2 cup	milk	125 mL
1/2 cup	half and half cream	125 mL
1/2 tsp.	salt	2 mL
1/4 tsp.	pepper	1 mL

- Melt the butter in a double boiler.

- Add the flour and stir until smooth. Gradually add the milk and cream. Add salt and pepper.

- Continue to cook, stirring constantly until the sauce is smooth and thick. Cook for 2 or 3 minutes longer.

- Just before mixture can come to a boil, remove it from heat. Adjust seasonings to taste.

- Place potatoes in an oven-proof casserole dish. Pour sauce over potatoes. Cover tightly and store in the refrigerator until Christmas Day.

- Before serving, heat thoroughly, uncovered, in the oven. Then cover to keep casserole hot when removed from oven. You may grate cheese on top, or add sprigs of fresh parsley before serving.

Step 8   *Christmas Day*

Make turkey dressing, using breadcrumbs, onion, and toasted hazelnuts finely chopped (all previously frozen), fresh savoury and melted butter. Stuff turkey.

While turkey is cooking, make a glaze of orange juice, diced pulp of two oranges and 1/2 cup (125 mL) of white sugar. During last hour of cooking, spoon glaze over bird frequently.

As soon as bird is cooked, remove from oven and pop in your pre-cooked casseroles to reheat.

Enjoy...

Taking the last minute hassle out of Christmas

1. Start early in the year…say January or February…and start buying then. I watch for the sales and try to take advantage of them. Remember, however, what you buy is what you keep! There are no exchanges on 11-month old goods or marked-down merchandise, so you have to be sure about sizes. I keep a list of names in a notebook in my purse, and by the end of summer or early in the fall season, the bulk of my shopping is done.

2. Start your gift wrapping on one of those wet and cold fall days when you have the house to yourself. I keep all my gift wrappings in a separate, easy-to-get-at box, and once a gift is wrapped I tuck it away on a shelf in a little-used closet. Just in case my memory fails me (as it is inclined to with greater frequency these days), I put a small, easily removed sticker (Post-it notes are great for this) on the end of the parcel, so I will know what is in it.

3. I keep all Christmas cards from the previous year in a shoe box. This serves two purposes, firstly as a reference for this year's card list. Subsequently, the cards that are suitable (ones with writing space on the front) are separated from their backs and used as gift tags. I got into this habit when I found that the really nice gift tags come in packages of four for the princely sum of $1.99! Pinking shears create a nice edge when using parts of the original card front (Christmas trees, Santas, and so on). If a hole is punched and the card attached to a gift by a ribbon, there is ample space to write a greeting on the underside of the attractive gift tag.

4. Visit your local wallpaper store frequently. You can often find rolls of very suitable wallpaper in a sale bin—it makes wonderful wrapping paper. I've been lucky in picking out winter scenes and children's paper; last year I even found a lovely, red velour roll. You can save a bundle this way, too!

5. When gift opening is underway on Christmas morning, I'm busy retrieving everyone's ribbons and bows. I put everything is a large paper bag, and when things are a bit quieter after the holidays, I iron the ribbon and roll it on toilet-paper rolls (saved, of course, for this purpose) and store them until the next Christmas season.

Things to do early to make Christmas cooking easier

- Make up a bag of bread crumbs and keep it in the freezer. You can do the same with cracker crumbs.

- Keep a bag of shredded cheddar cheese in the freezer. Use up all the leftover pieces of cheese this way, and toss a bit on a casserole, salad or open-faced sandwich.

- Chop onions and green peppers. Spread on a cookie sheet and freeze. When frozen, place in separate bags to store. These keep nicely for three months.

- Freeze dollops of whipped cream. Line a cookie sheet with waxed paper. Drop dollops of stiffly beaten cream and freeze. Gently place in a container and seal tightly. Minutes before using, remove as many dollops as you wish and pop them on your favourite dessert to finish thawing.

Here are some do-ahead *don'ts*

- Don't stuff a turkey, chicken, roast or fish ahead.

- Don't make egg sauces such as Hollandaise ahead. They do not reheat well.

- Don't bake, broil or fry fish ahead. It dries out quickly and gets tough.

- Don't include the potatoes when making stew if you intend to freeze the stew. They get watery and spongy. Instead, add the cooked potatoes when you are reheating the stew.

- Don't scrimp on freezer bags. Supermarket bags are not always airtight, allowing freezer burn.

Skating on the Bonnechere

We had been checking the ice on the Bonnechere River for days. It had started out as a thick, grey slush close to the shores and finally joined in the middle and turned a pure silvery white. By the time the mid-December cold snap hit Renfrew County with full force, the Bonnechere was frozen solid, except for a small portion at the shallow rapids. The river was not deep here (perhaps twenty-four inches) and as long as we lived in that part of the Valley, I never knew that twelve-foot square patch to freeze over. But the rest of the river froze smooth and clear, and that year back in the 1930s, we'd had little snow up to that point, so there wouldn't be much shoveling to do either.

Sunday was clear and cold, and we could hardly stand to sit in church until the service was over. Each of us, three brothers and a sister and my two young cousins, ate our dinner in one gulp and began to lace up and buckle on the array of skates which had to be divided between the seven of us. There were two pair of bob skates, and since my cousin Terry and I were the youngest and therefore had the smallest feet, we were tossed those hateful runners and told if we wanted to skate, those were the ones we had to wear. We were disgusted that Ronny, who wasn't much older than we were, but admittedly quite bigger, was to wear a pair of blades. We both thought better of complaining, however, because our mother had a way of dealing with complainers—they stayed out of the fun and were kept busy doing household chores.

We all wore our skates to the river; that was the only sensible thing to do as there was little chance of changing into them near the water, unless you wanted to sit in the snow to do so. As we headed out the door, Mother warned us to stay away from the open water. Her final words were, "Understand, Ronny?" Ronny was considered incorrigible back then, and my mother always anticipated that there would be trouble sooner or later, and she worked constantly at trying to ward it off before it happened. So, to my sister, Mother added, "Audrey, keep an eye on him."

We all hit the ice at the same time, and I remember being amazed at how adept Ronny was, but of course he had skated many times before in Montreal. He did fast turns, sudden stops which made the ice chips fly into the air, and then he taunted us by skating within a hair's breadth of the open water. Audrey screamed at him to stay away, but she might as well have been talking to the snowbank. He completely ignored her. He came barreling down the river, took an abrupt turn sideways and the ice flew over his head as he came to a sudden stop just a few feet from where the Bonnechere was flowing, open and black. Each time he charged down the river he seemed to go closer to the opening, and it was obvious that he was delighting in making Audrey's life miserable.

Finally the inevitable happened. Just a hair's breadth too close to the water once too often, and he skated as smooth as you please right into the hole. Of course, he was in no danger of drowning because the water was so shallow going over the rocks, but he screamed like someone going down in the *Titanic*. Audrey crawled on her stomach as close as she could get and stretched her arm out as far as she could reach. We could hear the ice snapping under her.

Ronny was hanging on for dear life, and his roars could be heard in Renfrew, I'm sure. Finally someone eased the shovel out over the ice and he clung to it while he scrambled out. Fortunately for Ronny, the house was only a field away, and between Audrey and my older brother, they were able to carry his stiff-clad body home. The rest of us stayed at the river and this further infuriated Ronny who was demanding that we all go home with him.

When we finally called it a day and made our way to the house, we could see his face in the kitchen window looking like a thundercloud. And when we went into the house we could see that Mother had put him into warm flannelette pyjamas belonging to one of my brothers. The legs of the pyjamas trailed on the floor, and the sleeves were about a foot too long. He looked so forlorn that for a moment I forgot that he had broken every rule in the book on the Bonnechere River. But then his tongue shot out a mile, and I saw that he was eating a piece of bread and jam, which we certainly were not allowed to do an hour before supper. He didn't deserve my pity, and I put my sympathy behind me and did something I rarely did and certainly not if my mother was looking. I stuck my tongue out, too, and crossed my eyes for good measure.

❧ German Apple-Sausage Supper ❧

1 lb.	pork sausage, cut into 1" (3 cm) pieces	450 g
1	large onion	1
4	large cooking apples, peeled and chopped	4
1 tbsp.	curry powder	15 mL
3 tbsp.	flour	45 mL
14 oz. can	evaporated milk	398 mL
1/2 cup	water	125 mL
4 cups	cooked hot rice	1L

- Fry sausage pieces until cooked; drain off fat, leaving 3 tbsp. (45 mL) in the pan.

- Add onion and cook until tender; add apples, stirring often until tender.

- Remove from heat and stir in curry powder mixed with flour, then milk and water.

- Cook slowly until thickened.

- Serve on hot rice.

Serves 4-6.

❧ Cabbage Rolls in Lemon Sauce ❧

1	medium head of cabbage	1
	boiling water	
1 lb.	ground beef	450 g
2	onions, chopped	2
1 cup	uncooked, long-grain rice	250 mL
1/8 tsp.	salt	.5 mL
1/8 tsp.	pepper	.5 mL
1/8 tsp.	oregano	.5 mL
	water to cover cabbage rolls	
2	eggs, beaten	2
	juice of 2 small lemons	

- Separate leaves of cabbage carefully and drop 8 into boiling water for approximately 2 minutes. Drain leaves one at a time.

- Mix beef with onions, rice, salt, pepper and oregano.

- Place 1/4 cup (50 mL) of the meat mixture on each cabbage leaf and roll up the leaves, tucking in the ends.

- Arrange in casserole and cover with water.

- Cover and bake at 350° F (180° C) for 40 minutes.

- Remove the lid, drain liquid and reserve.

- Put eggs and lemon juice in a small saucepan and simmer over low heat, adding cabbage juice a little at a time until sauce is smooth and thickened. Pour over cabbage rolls.

Serves 4-6.

❧ Hearty Ground Beef and Potato Casserole ❧

1	clove of garlic	1
2 tbsp.	oil	30 mL
1 1/2 lbs.	lean, ground beef	675 g
1	bay leaf, crumbled	1
1 tsp.	ground sage	5 mL
1 tsp.	salt	5 mL
1/8 tsp.	pepper	.5 mL
6 cups	thinly sliced, raw potatoes	1.5 L
1 cup	sliced onions	250 mL
2 tsp.	salt	10 mL
2	tomatoes, thinly sliced	2

- Cook garlic in oil for 5 minutes, then discard garlic. Add ground beef, bay leaf, sage, salt and pepper. Brown meat lightly.

- Remove the meat and brown the potato slices, stirring often and gently.

- Add onions and salt.

- In a greased 2-quart (2 L) casserole, alternate the layers of potatoes and meat, then the tomatoes, finishing with the potatoes and tomatoes.

- Cover and bake at 375° F (190° C) for 1 hour or until the potatoes are tender.

Serves 4-6.

❧ Quick New Brunswick Stew ❧

2 slices	bacon	2 slices
2 lbs.	boneless beef chuck or stewing beef	900 g
1	large onion, chopped	1
1	clove of garlic, minced	1
1-28 oz. can	tomatoes	796 mL
2 tsp.	salt	10 mL
1/4 tsp.	pepper	1 mL
1 cup	water	250 mL
1-16 oz. bag	frozen lima beans	500 g
1-16 oz. bag	frozen corn	500 g
2	fresh tomatoes, cut in wedges	2

- Cut the bacon in small pieces and cook in a large, heavy skillet or iron pot with a lid.

- Cut meat into 1" (3 cm) cubes.

- Add meat to the bacon, and brown slowly on all sides.

- Add onion and garlic and cook for 1 minute. Add canned tomatoes, salt and pepper and 1 cup (250 mL) of water.

- Cover and simmer for 1 1/2 hours, or until the meat is tender.

- Add lima beans and corn; cover and simmer for 15 minutes or until the beans are tender, adding more water if necessary.

- Stir in the fresh tomatoes and heat through.

Serves 6. This recipe may be doubled or tripled for a crowd.

The Nicest Christmas Tree

When my mother moved to the farm in the backwoods of Ontario after living for eighteen years in the heart of New York, she made a valiant attempt at keeping in touch with her beloved city, if not physically, at least in heart and spirit. It was Christmas, and the Depression was carrying on its quiet war all around us, but mother was able to bring to that isolated farm the joy of the season and to build for us a legacy of fond memories.

The spruce tree had been cut for several days before and it was hauled into the summer kitchen. We five children watched as our father took the broom to the branches to dislodge every last clump of snow which clung stubbornly to its bows. All eight feet of it was then dragged into the parlour. "In New York we always had the tree in the window so that people could see it from outside," Mother said. Father paused for just a moment, "And who do you think is going to see the tree from outside—the cows maybe?" So the tree was planted in a corner in a washtub of sand, and chicken wire anchored it to the wall and ceiling.

For weeks we had been hearing what a lean Christmas it was going to be. The leanest yet. There would be little money for toys, and certainly no money for tree decorations. We had made popcorn balls and paper links and these we hung on the tree, but it was bare beyond belief. We surveyed it sadly, but then our mother vanished upstairs and brought down what she called an under-the-bed box. It was, in fact, a large coat box, with *Gimbles* written across it in bold letters, and all we knew about it was that it was "private," and under no circumstances were we to go into it.

We gathered around the tree and watched as Mother carefully lifted the lid. Inside were all the decorations she had brought with her from New York. They weren't elaborate, but there were pieces of fruit and vegetables made of felt and embroidered in silver thread, and for the top of the tree, a white angel with outstretched arms and a cherub face. They had been wrapped carefully in a copy of the *Philadelphia Inquirer*, my mother's favourite newspaper, and when she laid them out on the table we thought they were the most beautiful ornaments we had ever seen.

We wanted to know why they had not been brought out in past years. Mother then told us that there seemed to be no need for them before, but *that* particular year had been a struggle and she knew that Christmas was going to be a lean one. "It seemed to be the right year for the New York decorations to come out of hiding," she said. After the last one was hung we stood back and admired the sight. We were sure it was the nicest Christmas tree in Renfrew County.

Later Mother went to the sideboard and got out her harmonica and settled herself into the old rocking chair. This was our cue to sit around her knee on the floor. She would give the harmonica a few sharp raps on the palm of her hand and run it up and down the scale just "to make sure all the notes were still there," as she'd say with a big wink. We sang Christmas carols—all the old favourites—and even though the song had nothing whatsoever to do with the Christmas season, my mother ended the singsong, as she always did, with "The Sidewalks of New York"—a final tribute to the city she had left behind.

Santa

No one thought it strange that the Montreal cousins chose to be with us over the holidays that year. Aunt Helen had come early, and Uncle Herby had just joined us a few days before Christmas.

The talk at our house was that Santa was on his way, and the reason I knew that for a fact was because I had been especially good, which was more than I could say for my cousin Ronny. He teased his younger brother Terry, and caused havoc at the school concert, when he called Marguerite a bad name which I can't even repeat now so many years later.

Finally it was Christmas Eve day. Supper, as usual, was a combination of Father's favourite German foods, and Mother's French Canadian specialties. We were as stuffed as the big turkey sitting out on the table in the summer kitchen ready to be popped into the oven just before Mother went to bed.

I used to think I liked Christmas Eve almost as much as I liked Christmas Day, especially when we had company like the Montreal cousins. Mother had taken out her harmonica, and Father had lit the candles on the Christmas tree with instructions that no one was to go near it but him. The threat of the whole place going up in smoke was enough to make us all behave.

We were taking a breath between singing carols, when Ronny piped up that he had no idea what we were waiting around for. If it was a visit from Santa we were all going to be sadly disappointed, because he knew for a fact that Santa was just imaginary. Well Terry, fortunately, had no idea what the word imaginary meant, so he wasn't the least bit fazed over the news. But I was devastated, and I looked to Mother for reassurance. She just nodded and said, "We'll see."

I had little heart left for the singing. This was the first time I had been told outright that Santa may just be imaginary. At eight years of age, I had questions, but I certainly wasn't going to rub out Santa with a simple statement from my cousin Ronny. After all, hadn't Santa always been especially good to me? No, I thought, Ronny has to be telling another one of his whoppers.

The evening wore on. We children were always allowed to stay up much later than usual on Christmas Eve, and only when we younger ones started to nod off, did Mother herd us off to bed. I looked at the old gingerbread clock on the kitchen wall. It was almost nine o'clock. The last time I had been up that late was when I had the measles, and old Mrs. Beam was giving me an onion treatment.

At the stroke of nine, we heard bells. We all stopped dead in our tracks. There was a clatter at the kitchen door and it was flung open hitting a chair behind it and sending it flying. And there, filling the whole doorway was Santa, red suit, beard and all. I thought I was going to explode, and Ronny…well, Ronny was so taken by surprise that he just about fell off his chair.

Santa came into the kitchen carrying a big grain sack. He reached in and handed each of us an orange, and then gave us all a little parcel which we weren't to open until after he had gone. He had a high, squeaky voice, not at all like I thought Santa would sound. Mother went over and gave his wide girth a hug, and Father and Uncle Herby shook his hand. We children just stood in awe. There was no attempt to close the kitchen door, and great gusts of winter air flowed in, but no one seemed to care.

Audrey asked him with a giggle, which I thought at the time was very disrespectful, if he would like a cookie and some tea. Father said he thought Santa would probably like a drink of homemade wine better, and he gave Uncle Herby a big wink which *I* noticed, but no one else seemed to see.

Santa said that would be wonderful, and he took the tumbler from Father and swallowed the wine in one, long gulp. And then, in the same squeaky voice, he said that he must be off, he had hundreds of homes to call on. Ronny, Terry and I followed Santa to the door and went out on the back step to wave him off. This was the most wonderful experience of my life, and I couldn't wait to tell Ronny when the door closed how mistaken he had been about Santa.

Santa climbed into the cutter which had brought him all the way from the North Pole, gave the horse a slap on its flank with the reins, shook the bells he had in his hands, and circled the yard, passing right by the kitchen door. We were still waving as he rounded the path, Ronny once again a believer. As the horse's hooves crunched on the snow, and Santa passed the door standing up, leaning over the seat and waving good-bye, I read the printing on the back of the cutter. It was as plain as day. Printed in white letters on the black paint, it said Renfrew County Mailman, Route 6.

I went to bed thinking Santa had borrowed the sleigh from Mr. Briscoe, but in my heart I knew Ronny had been right all along.

Christmas with Father

I always felt very special this time of year, and it wasn't only because I was the youngest of the five children. Although I suspect that fact did play a part in my feelings. I thought I probably got more Christmas gifts than did anyone else, even though they were of the simplest kind. While my sister and brothers got homemade mitts and scarves, and perhaps a shirt or blouse made out of something which had come in the hand-me-down box from Aunt Lizzie, I often found a little game under the tree, or some doll's clothes—clothes made from material that looked remarkably like the flannelette or broadcloth Mother kept wrapped in tissue paper in the trunk upstairs in the hall.

But I felt very special because, it seems to me now, Father spent more time with me during the Christmas season than he did with any of the other children. Instead of hiding behind the *Ottawa Farm Journal* at night sitting in the rocking chair by the cookstove, he would pull me onto his knee and tell me stories of when he was a little boy, and he would teach me nursery rhymes in German, which unfortunately I have long since forgotten. I felt so close to him at this time, and I would often tell myself that he probably liked me better than my brothers or sister. After all, he never took any of them onto his knee. Now, the fact that they were much older and bigger and wouldn't fit on his knee was something I chose not to consider.

He may have been working in the bush all day, coming home exhausted and soaked to the skin, but at Christmas he always took extra time to spend with me, whom he simply called, "the baby."

And when Christmas Eve rolled around, the excitement was at fever pitch in our old log house by the time we had finished eating Mother's tourtière, drinking hot chocolate, and singing carols while Mother belted out the tunes on the harmonica. I would look over at my father waiting in anticipation for the signal.

Bedtime would be coming soon. I had just learned to tell the time, and the hands on the gingerbread clock told me it would soon be time to go to bed. But Father had started a tradition with me when I was very young, and I knew there was one more ritual he and I would be going through before it was time to say evening prayers.

Without saying a word, he would ease me off his knee and head for the coat hook at the back door. I would follow him. No need for him to tell me what was in store. He would take the lantern from under the bench and light the wick. I would be struggling into my coat and pulling on my galoshes, and looking over at my brother Emerson with a smug look on my face, as if to say, "See…it's just Father and me…you're not included." Emerson would choose to do something else as if it didn't matter a bit to him, while all the time I felt in my heart he was being consumed with envy.

Father and I would head to the barn. I would walk tightly behind him, stepping into his footsteps in the snow. We'd go into the barn, warm and dank, and the lantern would barely light our way.

Then I'd see all the cow stalls, and I would once again be filled with wonder at the sight before me. Father would say, "See, I told you so." And there would be all the cows, every last one of them, lying down in their stalls. Father would once again tell me how, on Christmas Eve, the cows would instinctively know to lie down on the straw. He said no one could explain it. If we went into the barn any other time of the year, some may be down, but certainly many would be standing, chewing their cud. On Christmas Eve, something told the cows to lie down, just like in the Bible story we read every December in Sunday School.

Once again I would marvel at this miracle. Father and I would walk down behind the cows, and they would turn their heads and look at us and stay down on the straw. Father said as long as he could remember, he had come to the barn every Christmas Eve with his father, and he would see the cows down as if they, too, were waiting for the miracle.

I hoped then that things would never change. That always my father and I would go out to the barn on Christmas Eve and see this wonder…just the two of us.

The Doll

I first saw the doll in early December in the window of the dime store in Renfrew. I thought she was the most beautiful thing I had ever seen. I only liked dolls which looked like babies, not those that had pompadour hairdos and long crinoline gowns. This one had a round infant's face with two little teeth showing between ruby red lips, and bright blue eyes which closed when she was put down.

I went into the store that Saturday and asked the lady behind the counter if I could look at the doll. She took it out of the window, and I cradled it in my arms. Its body was soft and cuddly, and I wanted it so much I hurt inside. I handed it back knowing that I would never have it.

When we got home to Northcote that afternoon, to the farm which was suffering under the ravages of the Depression years like every other farm around us, I told my mother about the doll and said I wanted it more than anything else in the world. For the hundredth time she explained the Depression to me, saying that there was enough money for one toy that year, and the doll was much too expensive.

It was then that my father spoke up. "If there's any spare cash, it'll go towards a pair of new galoshes for your mother. This pair won't take many more patches." Father was working at the bench near the door in the kitchen. He had the tools that he used for fixing holes in the inner tubes of the old Model T. He was busy scraping my mother's galoshes with the little tin can with the rough holes in one end to make the spot ready for the piece of rubber he was about to glue on. He held the black rubber galosh high in the air. "I can't remember when these were bought, but they'll never see another winter. I think if Santa has any heart, he'll put a new pair under the tree for your mother." "Now, Dad," Mother said, "I'm sure you can fix those up just fine." I did my best to put the doll out of my mind, but even when I scrunched my eyes up tightly at night I could see her with her golden curls and her little flannelette nightgown. She was so real to me, I often felt I could reach out in the darkness and touch her.

Even though we had to go to Renfrew several times before Christmas, I didn't go near the dime store again. I thought I couldn't bear to see that she would no longer be in the window, but in someone else's home waiting for another little girl on Christmas morning.

My memories of Christmas mornings back in the 1930s are a jumble of mental pictures of us rushing to finish up the chores and of hurried breakfasts—we always had to eat before we got to look at the Christmas tree. Then we would tear into the parlour, fall to the floor in a circle around the tree while Father handed out the presents. That morning, there were the usual hand-knit mittens, my stocking with an orange in the toe, a book (always there was a book) and a game of Chinese Checkers. The doll was not there, as I was sure it wouldn't be.

Then my father reached deep behind the tree and pulled out a long box. He made a great show of not being able to make out the writing. "I think it says Mary, but I'm not sure," he said. "Better open it and see." I tore into the box and inside, lying on a little flannelette sheet which matched the pyjamas my mother had made for me in the fall, was the beautiful doll. I was so happy, I thought I was going to burst, and my mother and father were smiling, too. I don't ever remember being so ecstatic over a Christmas gift. I held her all morning, and even hated to part with her long enough to go to church. But Mother assured me she would be perfectly safe on my bed until we returned from the Christmas service.

When we were getting dressed in our coats and hats, it was only then that I noticed my mother reach down and pick up her old galoshes (patches on top of patches), give them a quick dust off with her gloves and put them on. She saw me looking. I felt so stricken, but then she said, "I can always get a pair of galoshes, but we might never find a doll as pretty as that one again."

At that time in my life, the reasoning was sufficient to make things right with my world. It was a bittersweet Christmas I shall never forget.

Christmas Menu II

Vegetable Cocktail
Roast Turkey with Make-Ahead Dressing
Green Bean Bake
Turnip Bake with Brown Sugar and Apples
Red Cabbage for a Change
Walnut Cranberry Pie

❧ Vegetable Cocktail ❧

- In blender, mix two stocks chopped celery, 2 ripe tomatoes, 1/2 green pepper.

- Chop until very soupy. Add freshly ground pepper and a bit of salt to taste.

- Pour 1 large can of tomato juice into a pitcher. Stir in puréed vegetables.

- Add a few drops of garlic juice. Chill thoroughly. Pour into glasses and top with chopped celery leaves.

❧ Make-Ahead Turkey Dressing ❧

- Buy a loaf of unsliced bread. Break into small pieces, or if you prefer, break it down in your blender.

- Spread the bread pieces on a large cookie sheet.

- Dry in a 300° F (150° C) oven for 10 minutes.

- Let cool and place in a plastic bag and freeze.

- The day before using, melt 1/2 cup (125 mL) butter, add 1 cup (250 mL) of raisins, 1 finely chopped apple and 1 chopped onion.

- Place in a sealed container in the refrigerator.

- Remove frozen bread pieces from freezer an hour before stuffing the turkey. Blend with raisin mixture. Add a few tablespoons of cream and toss lightly. Add sage to taste.

- Stuff bird lightly; do not pack stuffing into cavity.

☙ Green Bean Bake ☙

2 lbs.	fresh green beans	900 g
1	celery stalk, chopped	1
2/3 cup	butter	150 mL
4 tbsp.	cooking oil	60 mL
2 tbsp.	chopped onion	30 mL
2 tbsp.	chopped parsley	30 mL
2 oz.	flour	55 g
2 cups	milk	500 mL
8 oz.	medium or old cheddar cheese	250 g
	salt and pepper to taste	
4 tbsp.	breadcrumbs	60 mL
5	eggs	5

- Preheat oven to 425° F (220° C).

- Prepare beans and blanch for 5 minutes in salted water. Drain well.

- Melt half the butter with oil in a frying pan and brown celery, onion and parsley.

- Add beans. Cover and simmer on low heat for 10 minutes.

- Meanwhile melt the remaining butter in a saucepan.

- Stir in the flour, cook for 2 minutes, then gradually add milk.

- Stir and simmer until thick.

- Grate cheese and add to milk with salt and pepper.

- Grease a baking dish (a tube pan is particularly nice for this recipe) and coat on bottom and sides with breadcrumbs.

- Drain bean mixture and fold into sauce.

- Mix in lightly beaten eggs. Spoon into baking dish.

- Place dish in roast pan with hot water and bake for 25 minutes.

- Reduce heat to 400° F (200° C) and bake for 10 additional minutes.

- Let stand for 5 minutes, then invert on serving dish.

Note: This dish can be made in advance and frozen before being removed from pan. Reheat at 300° F (150° C) for 30 minutes after thawing. Then invert on serving plate.

❧ Turnip Bake with Brown Sugar and Apples ❧

- Cook two large turnips to serve 8 people. Drain well, and dry for a few minutes on the burner.

- Using a food processor, purée turnips (or mash thoroughly, then mix with a hand mixer).

- Add a bit of melted butter, and salt and pepper to taste.

- Put half of the turnips into a casserole. Add 3 or 4 thinly sliced and peeled apples on top of turnips.

- Dot with butter and brown sugar.

- Add the remaining turnips. Top with soft buttered breadcrumbs.

- If desired, sprinkle lightly with garlic salt.

- Bake at 325° F (160° C) for 1 hour.

- Cool slightly, wrap tightly and freeze.

Note: This casserole can be made and cooked two days in advance of serving. Refrigerate and reheat for 30 minutes before serving.

❧ Red Cabbage for a Change ❧

This recipe should serve 6-8 people. But because it is so good and very different, don't count on it stretching beyond 4! It's great to serve at Christmas because of its colour.

1	red cabbage, shredded	1
1 cup	water	250 mL
1/4 cup	vinegar	50 mL
1/3 cup	butter	75 mL
1/2 cup	brown sugar	125 mL
3/4 tsp.	salt	3 mL
1/2 tsp.	nutmeg	2 mL
4	cooking apples	4

- Combine all ingredients except apples in a large pot. Bring to a boil.

- Turn down the heat and allow to simmer for approximately 30 minutes, stirring several times.

- Peel, core and quarter the apples. Add them to the cabbage mixture and allow everything to cook an additional 30 minutes, or until most of the liquid has evaporated and the apples are tender.

❧ Walnut Cranberry Pie ❧

This is a super easy pie to make when holiday time is so limited. It looks wonderful and the taste is very different. It goes well with a buffet meal.

3 1/2 cups	fresh cranberries	875 mL
1/2 cup	light raisins	125 mL
3/4 cup	chopped walnuts	175 mL
1 1/2 cups	white sugar	375 mL
3 tbsp.	flour	45 mL
1/4 cup	corn syrup	50 mL
1 tbsp.	grated orange peel	15 mL
1/4 tsp.	salt	1 mL
2 tbsp.	butter, softened	30 mL
1	unbaked pie shell	1

- Preheat oven to 375° F (190° C).

- Grind cranberries and raisins together.

- Stir in the next 7 ingredients. Mix well.

- Pile the mixture into the unbaked pie shell.

- Bake for 45 minutes.

- Serve with a blob of whipped cream, or with maple-walnut ice cream.

A Short New Year's Eve

It was the first year I remember that my Montreal cousins were to be with us over the Christmas and New Year's holiday, and in spite of the fact that they would have had many more gifts had they stayed in the city, they elected to stay with us out at the farm. The snow was piled sky-high that year, and it was the kind of holiday season I recall with great fondness.

It wasn't the custom in that part of the Ottawa Valley to make too much fuss over New Year's Eve because, regardless of how late you stayed up, you still had to get out to the barn before daybreak and tend to the livestock, so that any thought of celebrating New Year's Eve soon lost its appeal when we considered what lay ahead of us in the morning.

Mother, however, having lived in New York City, missed the frivolity of the holiday season and often lamented that in her mind the Valley people certainly didn't do much about welcoming in a new year. She really didn't see that the cows would suffer that much if they weren't milked at the crack of dawn. But until that year when our cousins stayed over, Mother didn't belabour the point, and Father always won out with his reasoning that farm chores came first.

I don't remember whose idea it was that we all stay up to see in the new year. But sitting around the kitchen table with less than five hours left in the old year, someone said, since Ronny and Terry were with us, this might be a good year to stay up until midnight. Mother thought it would be a wonderful idea. Father thought it was the craziest notion he ever heard of and said, "It makes no matter to me if you're foolish enough to stay up to midnight, but I'll tell you one thing for sure, you'll all be up as usual at six." The thought of the late night, however, and the fun that lay ahead over-ruled everything else. It was decided we would all see in the new year, with the exception of my father, of course, who was already stoking the stove and having his final cup of green tea.

Mother got things off to a rousing start by leading us all in a singsong. All went well until Emerson decided he could sing in harmony. Of course, he threw everyone off-key, because even under ideal conditions, such as in the church choir, Emerson had a less-than-perfect singing voice. We all started to laugh at the discord, which threw him into a rage. Mother said we had had enough singing.

"Musical chairs" was a long-time favourite at any social gathering and we swung into the game after the singsong, with Mother on the harmonica. If you remember the game, you will know that there is always someone left without a seat when the music stops. The game had eliminated everyone but Ronny and Emerson, and they were running around the one chair so fast we could hardly see their legs moving. Mother had turned her back so as not to show any partiality.

Ronny soon found out that the only way to win was to pick up the chair and run with it, which certainly was a new twist and not exactly Emerson's idea of good sports-manship. What developed was the worst game of name-calling I had ever heard. The music stopped; Ronny dropped the chair and threw himself onto the seat with such an impact that the legs almost buckled; then Emerson flung himself on top of Ronny demanding that he be recognized as the winner. The screaming could be heard all over Admaston Township, I was sure, and except that Mother grabbed each by an ear, I think there surely would have been bloodshed.

It took Father about ten seconds to make it to the bottom of the staircase where he stood in his fleece-lined long-underwear, with one arm high in the air shouting,

"Enough! Enough! To bed, all of you! Can't a man get any rest around here, with daylight just around the corner?" Mother was putting her harmonica back in its blue velvet box, and it looked as if she was actually relieved that he had intervened.

When we climbed the stairs for bed that night, I noticed that the old gingerbread clock on the shelf in the kitchen said half-past eight. Our New Year's Eve party had lasted exactly forty-five minutes.

111

❧ Bacon Onion Appetizers ❧

These are wonderful to have on hand, because they freeze so well.

1/3 cup	butter, softened	75 mL
1/2 cup	very finely chopped onion	125 mL
8 slices	crisp, cooked bacon, crumbled	8 slices
2 tbsp.	chopped fresh parsley	30 mL
2 cans	refrigerated crescent rolls	2 cans

- Combine the first 4 ingredients and mix thoroughly.

- Unroll crescent rolls and separate into 8 rectangles…press firmly to seal the perforations.

- Spread the butter mixture evenly over dough.

- Roll up each rectangle, beginning with the shortest end. Pinch to seal.

- Cut each into 4 slices. Place on an ungreased cookie sheet and flatten a bit with the blade of a kitchen knife.

- Bake at 375° F (190° C) for about 15 minutes or until golden.

Makes 32 appetizers.

To freeze: Bake only until a light golden brown. Cool and freeze. To serve, thaw and place on a baking sheet and bake at 375° F (190° C) for 7 to 8 minutes.

❧ Top-of-the-Stove Duck ❧

5 to 6 lb.	duck	2.3 to 2.7 kg
2 tbsp.	cooking oil	30 mL
1 large	onion, finely chopped	1 large
1 cup	chicken broth or stock	250 mL
1 tsp.	salt	5 mL
1/2 tsp.	pepper	2 mL
1/2 tsp.	garlic salt	2 mL
1 1/2 tsp.	paprika	7 mL
1 cup	tomato sauce	250 mL
1 cup	fresh mushrooms	250 mL
2 tbsp.	butter	30 mL
1/2 cup	sweet sherry	125 mL

- Brown the duck slowly on all sides in oil in a heavy Dutch oven. Turn it very carefully so that it browns evenly. Pour off the fat.

- Place a rack in the Dutch oven and set duck on top.

- Add onion, chicken broth, salt, pepper, garlic salt and paprika, then tomato sauce.

- Simmer on the stove, covered, for 1 3/4 hours or until the duck is fork-tender. Baste the bird frequently with the liquid during cooking.

- Remove the duck to a hot platter when cooked.

- Lift out the rack and add mushrooms (which have been sautéed in butter) and sherry to the contents of the pot. Heat and pour over the duck.

Serves 4 to 5.

⊛ Cranberry Layered Cake ⊛

1 1/2 cups	sifted all-purpose flour	375 mL
1 1/2 tsp.	baking powder (double-acting preferred)	7 mL
1/2 tsp.	salt	2 mL
1 cup	chopped fresh cranberries	250 mL
2 tbsp.	grated orange rind	30 mL
1/3 cup	chopped walnuts	75 mL
3/4 cup	light brown sugar, firmly packed	175 mL
1 tbsp.	flour	15 mL
1/3 cup	soft shortening	75 mL
1/2 cup	granulated sugar	125 mL
1	egg, unbeaten	1
1 tsp.	almond extract	5 mL
1/2 cup	milk	125 mL

- Heat oven to 350° F (180° C).

- Grease and flour an 8" x 8" x 2" (2 L) baking pan.

- Sift together flour, baking powder and salt.

- In a small bowl, combine the cranberries, orange rind, nuts, brown sugar and 1 tbsp. (15 mL) of flour; set aside.

- In a large mixing bowl, using an electric mixer at medium speed, cream the shortening, gradually adding sugar, and beat until light and fluffy.

- Add the egg and almond extract and beat well.

- With mixer at low speed, add the flour mixture alternately with milk, beginning and ending with the flour mixture. Blend thoroughly after each addition.

- Spread half of the dough in the prepared pan. Top with half of the reserved cranberry mixture, spread remaining dough over the top of the cranberry mixture, then dot with the remaining cranberry.

- Bake for approximately 15 minutes or until done. Cut into squares and serve warm.

Serves 9.

☙ Russian Coffee ❧

In her later years, after moving away from the farm and into town, my mother would serve this icy-cold beverage for guests popping in between Christmas and New Year's Day. It became a favourite yuletide treat in our family. I have no idea why it was called Russian coffee; I do know you have to be a real coffee lover to enjoy it! This recipe makes one serving, so just increase it to serve as many people as you want.

1/3 cup	strong coffee, cooled	75 mL
1 tbsp.	powdered sugar	15 mL
1 tsp.	vanilla	5 mL
1/3 cup	light cream	75 mL
	ice cubes	

- Combine coffee, sugar and vanilla in a cocktail glass. Stir until sugar dissolves. Stir in cream. Add ice cubes. Serve immediately.

Winter Memories

It doesn't take much for a memory to be triggered in my mind. A walk up our country road and the smell of burning wood tumbling from a chimney along the way causes my mind to flash back to those days in the 1930s when our very survival depended on the cookstove in the kitchen. If I close my eyes I see Father plugging the woodbox with logs, and the smells of burning cedar and spruce fill my nostrils. Hardwood was saved for the night fire. Or I see Mother in my mind's eye on the coldest day of the winter with the perspiration pouring off her face as she laboured over a steaming pot of potatoes with the masher, or hauled bubbling pies from the oven. The very fires along our country road remind me so much of that time in my life when the Findlay Oval, the only source of heat in the entire house, served so many purposes. It radiated warmth through a network of pipes that snaked through the rooms upstairs. A fine piece of chicken wire, hung over the warming closet, dried our wet mittens and hats, and a block of wood between the Findlay Oval and the back wall of the kitchen served as a resting place for our felt inner soles from our gum rubbers. And, of course, an open oven door holding a cretonne cushion provided a cosy and comfortable resting place for Father's stockinged feet as he read the *Ottawa Farm Journal* after supper at night.

Passing along this country road of today, and smelling the scent of horses in an enclosure, my mind careens back more than fifty-five years, and a jumble of wonderful, warm memories come tumbling out. I think of bright nights when Father would hitch up the flat-bottom sleigh, and with us resting our backs against a bale of hay, we would head across the fields, impassable in the summer, and go over to our neighbours' home for an evening of cards and music. I barely have to stretch my mind to bring up the sounds of the runners of the sleigh crunching along on the hard snow, and the soft clopping of the horses' feet as they searched out a path. How I loved the moonlit night and the ride across that twenty-acre field. We always played a game where we tried to count the stars, and sometimes we saw a shooting star which Mother always took as a sign of bad luck. But Father said that was sheer nonsense which took my fear away immediately.

Coming home was even better, especially when the Montreal cousins were with us. Bricks would be burning hot from sitting out for the evening on our neighbours' cookstove. They would be wrapped in grain bags or newspaper and placed at our feet for the ride back over the big field. And always Mother sat with her arms around young Terry and me. Ronny considered himself much too grown-up to be held, preferring to be at the back of the sleigh with my brothers. And by the time we pulled into the yard in front of our old log house, little Terry would be fast asleep and would have to be carried inside. The next morning he would vow he had been awake all the time.

Now, if I go further up our country road to the little bridge, I don't see McGibbons Creek, I see the Bonnechere River. My memory of skating on a cleared patch of ice fills me with a warmth that defies the cold of the day. I think of sitting on the fallen tree, and how patient my sister Audrey was as she tied and retied my skates until they were just right. And how, because I was the youngest in my own family, I was on the very end of the line for "crack the whip." Today I can still feel the sharp wind on my face as we cut across the Bonnechere, laughing, falling, licking the snow off our mittens, cosy warm, in oversized hand-me-down melton snowsuits.

And if I scrunch my eyes up tight I see my mother in the kitchen waiting for us to come home, with steaming hot chocolate in a white granite pot on the back of the stove, and ginger cookies to dip into it. I see all of us sitting around the big pine table, in nothing but our long-underwear, with no embarrassment, Audrey and my brothers and any number of neighbourhood children who had tagged along, laughing and reliving the day while our clothes dried out on chairs around the stovepipe.

Today when I see a young mother pulling her child in a 1990s sleigh, shiny red, with silver runners, I think of the homemade sleigh we loved, and the hours Father spent on it, getting the runners just right. I hope I can be forgiven for thinking my sleigh of the 1930s was nicer.

The smells and the sounds of winter today are like stepping stones, taking me back to another era…when the cares of the world belonged to someone else. And once again I feel cosy, wrapped in the warm memories of another time.

Recipe Index

Wishing you
and all of your
loved ones
many happy,
memorable
Christmases!